Navigating Academia

D1044301

Navigating Academia

Writing Supporting Genres

JOHN M. SWALES

CHRISTINE B. FEAK

VOLUME 4 OF THE REVISED AND EXPANDED EDITION OF
English in Today's Research World

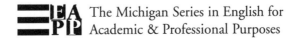 The Michigan Series in English for
Academic & Professional Purposes

Copyright © by the University of Michigan 2011
All rights reserved
Published in the United States of America
The University of Michigan Press
Manufactured in the United States of America

∞ Printed on acid-free paper

ISBN: 978-0-472-03453-6

2014 2013 2012 2011   4   3   2   1

No part of this publication may be reproduced, stored in a retrieval system, or transmitted in any form or by any means, electronic, mechanical, or otherwise, without the written permission of the publisher.

Acknowledgments

As ever, our first expression of gratitude needs to go to all those students and workshop participants who have responded so willingly and creatively to various drafts of the materials in this small book. We have also been able to incorporate many of the useful suggestions made by the two anonymous reviewers on an earlier version of this manuscript. The book also owes much to our invaluable research assistant, Dr. Vera Irwin, for her careful and critical readings of the evolving drafts, for assisting in getting the manuscript ready for the publisher, and for drafting much of the Online Commentary; more specifically, it was Vera who eventually resolved our long struggle to create an appropriate title for this volume by coming up with *Navigating Academia*. We are very grateful to Professor John Benfield for being able to use some of his material dealing with responding to reviewers, to PhD Comics for the first of the three cartoons, to Vivienne Hixon for allowing us to continue to use two of her illustrations, and to the *American Journal of Radiology* for permission to reproduce part of the Baumeister letter. And not least, we would like to offer our continuing appreciation to Kelly Sippell, Executive Acquisitions Editor for Applied Linguistics and ESL Titles, at the University of Michigan Press. Kelly's long-standing support for "Swales & Feak" advanced textbooks has made her a trusted collaborator and always a source of insight about what is happening in her area of expertise.

On a more personal level, John would like to thank Vi Benner, his partner for more than twenty years, for willingly coming to accept the fact that his official "retirement" from the University of Michigan would not mean stopping from going to the English Language Institute several times a week or spending many hours working at his computer in the basement. Chris, once again, would like to thank her family, Glen, Karl, and Angie, for their support and interest in this project. Their appreciation of her work is a great source of motivation.

JMS & CBF
Ann Arbor
January 2011

Grateful acknowledgment is given to the following authors, publishers, and individuals for permissions to reprint copyrighted material.

Dr. John Benfield for allowing us to incorporate and adapt materials he developed to help authors correspond with reviewers and editors.

Jorge Cham for "Piled Higher and Deeper" from www.phdcomics.com. Used with permission.

Dialogue, the Newsletter of the Society for Personality and Social Psychology for "sample cover letter for journal manuscript resubmissions: Dear Journal Editor, It's Me Again" by Roy F. Baumeister, copyright 1990.

Vivian Hixon for illustration on page 61.

Every effort has been made to contact the copyright holders for permission to reprint borrowed material. We regret any oversight that may have occurred and will rectify them in future printings of this volume.

Contents

General Introduction to the Volumes

John and Chris first started putting together the book that became *English in Today's Research World: A Writing Guide* (henceforth *ETRW*) in early 1998. The book was largely based on teaching materials we had been developing through the 1990s for our advanced courses in dissertation writing and writing for publication at the University of Michigan. Ten years later, that "research world" and our understanding of its texts and discourses have both changed considerably. This revised and expanded series of volumes is an attempt to respond to those changes. It also attempts to respond to reactions to *ETRW* that have come from instructors and users and that have reached us directly, or through Kelly Sippell, ESL Editor at the University of Michigan Press. One consistent feature of these comments has been that *ETRW* is somewhat unwieldy because it contains too many disparate topics. In thinking about a second edition, therefore, we have made the radical decision to break the original book into several small volumes; in addition, we offer a volume principally designed for instructors and tutors of research English and for those who wish to enter this growing field of specialization. We hope in this way that instructors or independent researcher-users can choose those volumes that are most directly relevant to their own situations at any particular time.

However, we do need to stress that many of the genres we separately deal with are inter-connected. Even if a literature review is originally conceived as a freestanding object, later it is typically reshaped as part of a research project or part of a grant application. Abstracts are always abstracts of some larger text. A conference talk may be based on a dissertation chapter and may end up as an article. Grant proposals lead to technical reports, to dissertations, and to further grant proposals. To indicate these inter-connected networks, a revised version of the genre network diagram (see Figure 1) we used in *ETRW* is appropriate and even more relevant to this multivolume series.

Figure 1. Open and Supporting Academic Genres

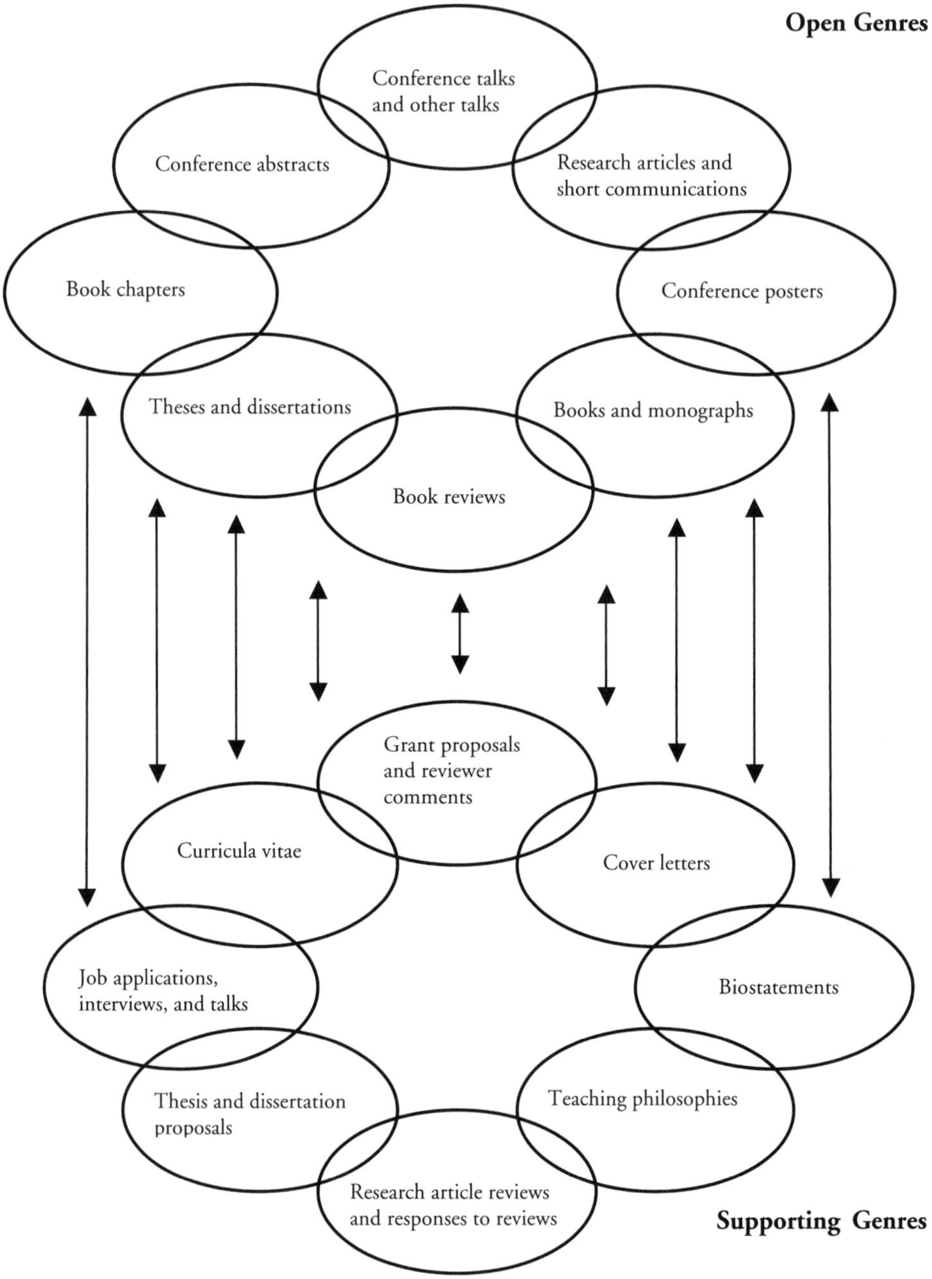

Open Genres

Conference talks and other talks

Conference abstracts

Research articles and short communications

Book chapters

Conference posters

Theses and dissertations

Books and monographs

Book reviews

Grant proposals and reviewer comments

Curricula vitae

Cover letters

Job applications, interviews, and talks

Biostatements

Thesis and dissertation proposals

Teaching philosophies

Research article reviews and responses to reviews

Supporting Genres

One continuing development in the research world has been the increasing predominance of English as the vehicle for communicating research findings. Of late, this trend has been reinforced by policy decisions made by ministries of higher education, universities, and research centers that researchers and scholars will primarily receive credit for publications appearing in English-medium international journals, especially those that are included in the Institute for Scientific Information (ISI) database. Indeed, in recent years, the range of "acceptable" publication outlets has often been further narrowed to those ISI journals that have a high impact factor (in other words, those with numerous citations to articles published over the previous three years). Selected countries around the world that have apparently adopted this kind of policy include Spain, the United Kingdom, China, Brazil, Malaysia, Chile, and Sri Lanka. Competition to publish in these high-status restricted outlets is obviously increasingly tough, and the pressures on academics to publish therein are often unreasonable. A further complicating development has been the rise and spread of the so-called "article-compilation" PhD thesis or dissertation in which the candidate is expected to have an article or two published in international journals *before* graduation.

The increasing number of people in today's Anglophone research world who do not have English as their first language has meant that the traditional distinction between native speakers and non-native speakers (NNS) of English is collapsing. A number of scholars have rightly argued that we need to get rid of this discriminatory division and replace NNS with speakers of English as a lingua franca (ELF) or speakers of English as an additional language (EAL). Today, the more valid and valuable distinctions are between senior researchers and junior researchers, on the one hand, and between those who have a broad proficiency in research English across the four skills of reading, writing, listening, and speaking and those with a narrow proficiency largely restricted to the written mode, on the other.

There have also been important developments in English for Academic Purposes (EAP) and allied fields. The relevant journals have been full of articles analyzing research English, often discussing as well the pedagogical consequences of such studies. This has been particularly true of studies emanating from Spain. Indeed, the first international conference on "Publishing and presenting research internationally" was held in January 2007 at La Laguna University in the Canary Islands.

The use of corpus linguistic techniques applied to specialized electronic databases or corpora has been on the rise. The number of specialized courses and workshops has greatly expanded, partly as a way of utilizing this new knowledge but more significantly as a response to the increasing demand. Finally, information is much more widely available on the Internet about academic and research English, particularly via search engines such as Google Scholar. As is our custom, we have made much use of relevant research findings in this and our other volumes, and we—and our occasional research assistants—have undertaken discoursal studies when we found gaps in the research literature. In this process, we have also made use of a number of specialized corpora, including Ken Hyland's corpus of 240 research articles spread across eight disciplines and two others we have constructed at Michigan (one of dental research articles and the other of research articles from perinatology and ultrasound research). We are also beginning to make use of the Michigan Corpus of Upper-level Student Papers (MICUSP), which became available in late 2009.

In this new venture, we have revised—often extensively—material from the original textbook, deleting texts and activities that we feel do not work so well and adding new material, at least partly in response to the developments mentioned earlier in this introduction. One concept, however, that we have retained from our previous textbooks is in-depth examinations of specific language options at what seem particularly appropriate points.

As this and other volumes begin to appear, we are always interested in user response, and so we welcome comments at either or both cfeak@umich.edu or jmswales@umich.edu.

Introduction to the Supporting Genres Volume

This volume is somewhat different from others in the series. The main difference resides in the fact that this volume focuses on the *supporting genres* that facilitate the more public genres (research papers, dissertations, conference presentations) that form the building blocks of an academic and/or research career. Examples of these supporting genres—all of which are covered in this volume—are Statements of Purpose for graduate school applications, letters of recommendation, responses to journal reviewers, and various kinds of email. One feature that these genres have in common is that they are largely hidden from public view; it is difficult to find examples of them in university libraries. Although guidance about these genres can increasingly be found on the Internet, this guidance is often too general to be helpful in your own particular situation. This is unfortunate because these genres are crucially concerned with what famous sociologist Erving Goffman called "impression management," in this case, managing the impression that you make on your reader. In almost all cases, you need to be seen as both a serious scholar, researcher, or instructor (whether beginning or getting established) and as a collegial but objective person. As a result, many of these academic communications need to be carefully considered, particularly with regard to the likely effect your communication will have on its intended recipients, who, more often than not, are established figures in your field (as with a job application letter). Because of the roles of these genres, this volume also differs somewhat from the others in that it is as much concerned with social academic practice as it is with more formal academic texts.

In our textbook writing over many years, we have occasionally given imagined or real expert reactions to student or junior scholar texts. The advantage of this is that it puts students in a new place by showing them how their texts may be perceived. Because of the nature of this volume, we have increased our use of this particular technique.

Although so far we have stressed what is distinctive about this volume, we also need to point out that our underlying pedagogical approach remains largely the same. For example, Figure 2 shows how these supporting genres are interconnected and form complex networks with the boxed "open"

Figure 2.

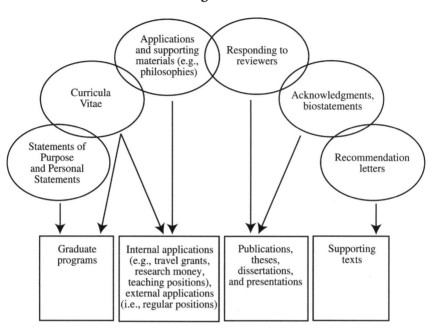

genres (such as publications and presentations) shown in the lower part of the figure.

Even so, the situated circumstances of each use of one of these supporting genres tends to be distinct; for instance, compare writing a letter of recommendation for an undergraduate research assistant in your research group to writing one for the group's director, who is being considered for promotion. For that reason, we have here focused on treating each genre in its own terms and with its own linguistic and rhetorical characteristics. In each case, we again have stressed the value of raising your consciousness about what is going on in this genre and why. For this, we have again opted for various kinds of text analysis as well as suggesting that there is much value in examining your own past practice and those of others that you can access. As usual, we have attempted to offer an interesting variety of tasks—whether working on your own or in a class setting—that further these objectives. In the end, we hope that users of this small volume will feel more "genre ready" as they contemplate sending a request email to a professor in some distant country, writing a tricky "teaching philosophy" statement as part of an academic job application, or writing a much simpler biostatement to accompany an article recently accepted for publication (congratulations!).

We have organized this book around the concept of a journey of entering graduate school, passing through it, and leaving it to take up an academic or research-oriented career. Obviously, any one individual at the time of opening the volume cannot be at all these stages at the same time. As a result, a PhD student might want to skip Section 1; on the other hand, a Master's student might focus on this section but leave some of the later material until another day. In a similar way, instructors adopting this volume will need to judge which sections and subsections will be most appropriate for their particular classes. For all users, *Navigating Academia* should be able to serve as a reference, not only for the present, but also for the future.

Navigating Academia is supported by an Online Commentary available at www.press.umich.edu/esl/compsite/ETRW/.

An Opening Orientation

AVERAGE TIME SPENT COMPOSING ONE E-MAIL

WWW.PHDCOMICS.COM

Reproduced with permission from *Piled Higher and Deeper*
by Jorge Cham (www.phdcomics.com).

This volume covers a lot of ground. So, in order to get some sense of the kinds of consideration that hold it together, we offer this short overview section. One way of doing this is via a questionnaire—a questionnaire designed to get you to think (and perhaps rethink) your attitude toward academic correspondence and its related genres.

Task One

How do you respond to these statements? Circle the numbers of your responses (1 = strongly disagree; 5 = strongly agree). If you have a partner, discuss your responses as you proceed.

1. Effective academic correspondence is as important as effective scholarly or research writing.   1   2   3   4   5

2. Creating and responding to emails well is useful, but not as important as making a good impression in face-to-face meetings.   1   2   3   4   5

3. I would always ask one of my professors for advice before submitting an important application (e.g., for a full-time job).   1   2   3   4   5

4. Letters of recommendation are easy to write because they are about other people.   1   2   3   4   5

5. The more senior the person, the more carelessly written his or her emails tend to be.   1   2   3   4   5

6. In application letters, the focus should be on what you can do for the organization you are applying to, not on what you have done in the past (for another institution).   1   2   3   4   5

7. Open (To Whom It May Concern) recommendation letters have very little value.   1   2   3   4   5

8. Spontaneous emails (those written using an email program) are typically fresher but less audience-sensitive than those composed using a word processing program and then copied and pasted into the message.   1   2   3   4   5

9. Subject lines in emails are more important than generally thought.   1   2   3   4   5

10. Colleagues are a better source of assistance with academic correspondence than the Internet.   1   2   3   4   5

Students in one of our current Writing for Publication classes completed the questionnaire, and their averaged responses are given. (Remember, the higher the score, the greater the agreement with the statement.) How do your scores compare?

1. 4.1
2. 2.3
3. 4.3
4. 1.4
5. 2.5
6. 3.1
7. 2.5
8. 2.5
9. 4.0
10. 3.9

As you can see, there was agreement with Statements 1, 3, 9, and 10; disagreement with Statement 4; and neutral or mixed responses to the others. So, the class did think that effective academic correspondence, getting advice from advisors, and choosing good email subject lines were all important. They also did not think that writing letters of recommendation is easy!

The Structure of Supporting Genres

The next introductory topic is the *rhetorical organization* of examples of supporting genres, which will be followed by a short section on questions of appropriate style. One well-known instance of the former is the different structure of "good news" letters (you got the job) and "bad news" letters (sorry, you didn't get the job). According to experts in business communications, the announcement of a successful outcome can come early in the letter, while in the "bad news" case, the reader should be prepared for rejection by various kinds of preceding explanation. These might include statements about the large number of applicants, the closeness of the decision given the quality of the candidates, or the seriousness with which the committee has considered the reader's application.

Another instance of differences in rhetorical organization can be seen in requests. Here are the two main possibilities for where to place the request (Kirkpatrick, 1991):

1. request followed by supporting reasons and/or justifications
2. reasons and/or justifications leading up to the request

1. What about yourself? Do you have a preference? Does your culture have a general preference? (According to Kirkpatrick, Chinese culture generally prefers the second one.)

2. Or do you think it all depends on the circumstances? For example, simple requests can be direct and up front, while major and imposing requests will need considerable preparation.

Task Two

Here are two versions of an email request; they differ principally in their structure. Which do you prefer, and why?

Text A

Dear Professor Swales,

I have been interested in your work for some time, and I am currently writing a thesis on the history of English for Specific Purposes in the Arab World. In this context, I have seen a reference to a 1983 volume on this topic, which you co-edited with Hassan Mustafa. I have looked for it here in Morocco, but in vain; I found it is not available. Would you be able to send me a copy? I am looking forward to hearing from you soon,

With respect

Ms Fatima Abdulla

Text B

Dear Professor Swales

Would you be able to send me a copy of the 1983 volume on English for Specific Purposes in the Arab World, which you co-edited with Hassan Mustafa? I have looked for it here in Morocco, but in vain; I found it is not available. I am currently writing a thesis on the history of English for Specific Purposes in the Arab World. I have been interested in your work for some time. I am looking forward to hearing from you soon.

With respect,

Ms Fatima Abdulla

Academic Correspondence Styles

Over the years and for a number of reasons, correspondence styles have become slowly and somewhat more informal. A hundred years ago, an academic job applicant might open the letter with something like:

a. The undersigned is extremely desirous of obtaining gainful employment with your esteemed institution. . . .

On the other hand, the academic job search remains a serious business today, and it is still unacceptable to use a highly informal and colloquial style such as:

b. Hi! I saw your recent advert, so I'm really keen on getting a job with your outfit. . . .

Most people expect a happy medium in academic correspondence—personal but quite formal:

c. I am writing to apply for your Assistant Professor position in the Department of Economics recently posted in *The Chronicle of Higher Education*. . . .

Task Three

Which of these concluding statements would you choose for an application cover letter?

    a. Thanks for reading my application & looking forward to hearing back soon.

    b. In closing, this applicant iterates his deep interest in the position and expresses his profound appreciation of your careful review of his case.

    c. Thank you for your consideration and looking forward to hearing from you in due course.

And the closing salutation? We have listed these in order from most formal to most informal. Where in the list would you place *Kind Regards, Yours Truly,* and *Cheers*?

    d. Yours faithfully

    e. Sincerely

    f. Warm regards

    g. Regards

    h. Best wishes

    i. Best

On a Lighter Note

We close this section with a parody that circulated on the Internet several years ago. You will remember that earlier we briefly discussed some of the components of standard job rejection letters, such as an expression of regret, a reference to the unexpectedly large number of applicants, and the use of evasive phrases like *does not meet our needs at this time.*

In what follows a rejected applicant pretends to get her "revenge," imitating the style and content of the typical "bad news" letter. There is always something to learn from good parodies about the characteristics of the originals. So enjoy!

Professor Charles E. Carpenter
Chair, Department of Social Physics

Dear Chuck,

Thank you for your letter of March 17. However, after careful consideration, I regret to inform you that I am unable to accept your refusal to offer me employment with your institution.

This year has been exceptional in that I have received an unusually large number of rejection letters. In such a circumstance, it has proved impossible for me to accept all refusals.

Despite your university's outstanding qualifications and previous experience in rejecting applicants, I find that your rejection does not meet with my needs at the present time. Therefore, I will initiate employment with your university at the beginning of the new academic year. I look forward to seeing you then.

Best of luck in rejecting future candidates.

Sincerely
Sophia P. Petros

Getting into Graduate School

Statements of Purpose and Personal Statements are typically one to two-page essays required as part of graduate student applications in the United States for master's and doctoral programs. These texts are now part of a complex set of application documents that also includes:

a. a CV (see pages 85–91)

b. a GPA transcript from your undergraduate school

c. Various test scores such as GRE® and TOEFL®

d. Two or three letters of recommendation

e. In many humanities and social science fields, a sample of your academic writing, such as a term paper.

At the time of writing, the situation in the United States with regard to these two genres is rather inconsistent. Some universities prefer the term *Statement of Purpose* (SOP) and some prefer the term *Personal Statement* (PS) while still expecting similar one to two-page essays from their applicants. On the other hand, according to recent research, more and more departments are increasingly expecting both! In these cases, of course, the two texts will have to be very different.

Elsewhere, as in the U.K., only one statement is usually required. Again, this is an important document. This quotation from Lancaster University (U.K.) is typical:

> This is an important section of the form as our admissions staff will use it to understand why you wish to study with us and what makes you a suitable candidate for the programme you have chosen.

Statements of Purpose

We will start with Statements of Purpose (SOPs). The SOP is a problematic genre to write for a number of reasons:

Reason 1. In contrast to many of the 'open' genres, it has been under-researched by applied linguists, apart from a 2004 special issue of the journal *Issues in Writing* and two recent articles in *English for Specific Purposes* (Ding, 2007; Samraj & Monk, 2008).

Reason 2. It is a significant part of the gatekeeping process for graduate school entry.

Reason 3. Due to different educational traditions and emphases in various parts of the world, some readers in the U.S. may have difficulty in interpreting and appreciating SOPs from international students.

Reason 4. The genre is challenging because, as Ding (2007) points out, most applicants are unfamiliar with the conventions of the genre and are (as yet) unfamiliar with the expectations of the disciplinary community they are hoping to enter.

Reason 5. Different strategies are needed for master's and PhD program SOPs.

Reason 6. The two current names for the genre (*Statement of Purpose* and *Personal Statement*) are both somewhat misleading.

We will comment on these issues in reverse order.

Reason 6. The SOP label tends to cause authors to overemphasize their anticipated future research projects and career trajectories, while the PS label tends to cause authors to overemphasize their past achievements. It is therefore necessary to think carefully about how best to balance stressing the value of past achievements and the validity and credibility of future aspirations.

Reason 5. Applicants to PhD programs need to demonstrate in some way that they have the intellectual resources and academic persistence to survive a typical five-year journey to a U.S. PhD. In contrast, master's applicants need to stress their professional involvement and their determination to acquire useful, practical skills within a relatively short time frame. (In consequence, a particular danger confronts those master's students going on to apply for a PhD because their personal statements should not suggest that they just want "more of the same" type of education.)

Reason 4. It is hard to get good examples that are both relevant and helpful for your own particular situation. Although general advice is increasingly available in manuals and on the Internet (Samraj & Monk, 2008), it can be misleading. For example, Brown (2004), in his study of applications for PhD psychology programs, showed that applicants in this field need to be aware of whether the departmental focus is primarily on academic research or clinical practice. Obviously, this kind of consideration is not generally applicable.

Reason 3. Our experience of reading SOPs and helping international students with their drafts suggests that different parts of the world have different priorities and so emphasize different things. These differences may still, in a globalizing world, reflect cross-cultural differences, but equally they may reflect different educational values. In effect, the following "moves" may not always have the positive effect on their U.S. readership that their authors are looking for:

> Some SOPs contain lengthy early educational histories and rely heavily on ranking data. For example, "My department is ranked as the fourth best in my country, and in my final undergraduate year I was ranked third out of 73 civil engineering students."
>
> Some SOPs contain appeals for sympathy and special consideration: "Despite my humble background, I have studied hard all my life, even when life was very difficult. Moreover, I am the youngest of eight siblings, only two of whom have jobs."
>
> SOPs may appear too modest and rely too much on the belief that "deeds speak louder than words": "As you can

see from my CV, I have done reasonably well at college, and I now feel I may be ready for graduate school."

Some SOPs try to cover all the bases by showing that the applicant is interested in everything a department has to offer. So a linguistics applicant might write, "I am interested in generative syntax, phonetic change, Jamaican creoles, cross-cultural semiotics, and neurolinguistics."

Reason 2. An SOP is not a simple document to create and will probably require several drafts. It is also important. One sensible piece of advice is to get the reactions of others to those drafts, such as teachers, fellow students, or more senior students and those already in a U.S. higher degree program. This provides an opportunity to test out whether you are making the right impression on your readers.

Reason 1. In the 2004 *Issues in Writing* on SOPs, Bekins, Huckin, and Kijak offer a move analysis of medical residency application statements, which they calculate was adopted in 60–70 percent of the effective texts:

> **Move 1: Hook** (a narrative to grab the reader's attention)
>
> **Move 2: Program** (why this particular specialization/location)
>
> **Move 3: Background** (evaluation of skills, landmarks of achievement)
>
> **Move 4: Self-promotion** (distinctive individual qualities)
>
> **Move 5: Projection** (personal professional goals/career trajectory)

Here is one of their winning hooks (from an application for medical residency in surgery):

I remember hearing the loud snap resonating across the field and having no doubt it was broken. Looking down at my forearm during the high school football game, the distal end dangling as both the left radius and ulna had been broken at midshaft. I felt certain I had experienced my last football event. . . .

As you can doubtless imagine, the application goes on to say that this fore-arm was fully mended by brilliant surgical intervention and thus the young man was inspired to follow a career in surgery.

A second example comes from an undergraduate of our acquaintance who graduated in 2006 in linguistics and then applied for an MA in applied linguistics at a leading British university. She opens with this rhetorically arresting mini-hook:

> The moment came on Friday, June 23rd, 2006, at precisely 5:25 PM. I was attending an applied linguistics conference. . . . (and then she goes on to write about the conference, and about many other things).

But at the end of her *final* paragraph, she returns to her "mysterious" opening sentence:

> As the conference went on, I set a challenge for myself: I would ask a question of one of the speakers about their presentation. When the final speaker stepped up to the podium, I knew this was my last chance . . . And so the moment arrived, that Friday afternoon; I stood up, took a deep breath, and crossed the line from observer to participant in the professional world of applied linguistics.

As you might have guessed, her application was also successful.

These two examples underscore the importance of a good start. In fact, the observational and interview data in the *Issues in Writing* volume discussed earlier indicate that the expert readers on admission committees rely to a considerable extent on first impressions—whether they are turned on or turned off by the opening paragraph. A wrong step here can be hard to recover from. For example, Barton, Ariail, and Smith found that "if the opening failed, either because it was not memorable or because it made no compelling connection to the profession, the readers skipped, skimmed, expressed criticism, and generally reacted negatively to the text" (2004, p. 109). But here we need to remember that these readers were working in a medical school context. Elsewhere, different criteria may apply, but a generally useful question to ask yourself is: *What is there about my statement that the reader will remember?*

Task Four

This task offers a sample SOP from a master's student (here called Gene) applying for a PhD program in Chemical Engineering. Since it is fairly long, we have added short numbered paragraph headings to help you through it. We have also added sentence numbers for ease of reference. Now read the SOP and the discussion between the author and his writing tutor that follows. Then respond to the questions that have been inserted within the discussion.

Statement of Purpose

(1) Engineering today in general and at your university

① Contemporary engineering requires a comprehensive approach in creating new ideas and concepts. ② Various engineering disciplines are essential to solving the most sophisticated technical questions. ③ As such, I believe that it is crucial to combine my Mechanical Engineering background with Chemical Engineering in order to study my chosen area of energy conversion and storage systems. ④ The resources available in the PhD program in Chemical Engineering at the University of _____ will help me attain my ambition to become an interdisciplinary expert in the field.

(2) My background in engineering and my current interests

⑤ I believe that gaining in-depth knowledge in Chemical Engineering is indispensable to creating an efficient fuel cell system. ⑥ As an undergraduate Automotive Engineering major, I was deeply fascinated with developing an environmentally friendly energy system in automobiles. ⑦ This interest prompted me to pursue my Master's in Mechanical Engineering to gain access to numerous related research studies. ⑧ During my Master's, I have become more interested in a specific area of an alternative energy source—fuel cells and batteries—than a powertrain system in general. ⑨ This area of interest has guided me through my academic pursuit ever since.

(3) Why I want to do a PhD in Chemical Engineering

⑩ The interest, however, encountered limitations caused by the heavy emphasis on a theoretical approach in Mechanical Engineering and my lack of understanding of electrochemical reactions in Chemical Engineering. ⑪ My Master's research project under Prof. XXX was theory-oriented since I mainly conducted model development of a PEM fuel cell based on physics and its simulation. ⑫ And yet, this theoretical approach proved insufficient to attain the research objectives. ⑬ A theoretical approach seemed only "theoretical" to me without results from relevant experiments. ⑭ In addition, I realized the need for expertise in Chemical Engineering for an integrated approach to the fuel cell system. ⑮ Although I read a number of journals in the field of electrochemistry, it was hard to connect transport phenomena in fuel cells with relevant electrochemical reactions without a knowledge of Chemical Engineering.

(4) My special interests in fuel cells

⑯ Through this process, I have grasped the significance of combining my Mechanical Engineering background with Chemical Engineering. ⑰ Chemical Engineering's focus on experiments will assist me in improving my lack of experiments in my interested field. ⑱ Besides, expertise in Chemical Engineering will help me better understand the process of catalytic reactions coupled with thermal-fluid transport. ⑲ This knowledge in thin film and catalysis process will be an indispensable asset to produce a stable and efficient fuel cell performance.

(5) Why your department is the best for me

⑳ The Chemical Engineering department at the University of _____ is renowned for its excellence in my area of interest and for being a close-knit community. ㉑ Along with its specific research interest in the field of Energy and Environment, the department also has faculty members who share similar research interests to mine. ㉒ Prof. XXX, Prof. XXX, and Prof. XXX in the department all demonstrate their interest in the field of electrochemical fuel cells. ㉓ I was also impressed with the department's intimate environment. ㉔ From my previous ChE 602 class, I witnessed the dynamic interaction and care between students and faculty members that will be definitely helpful to my adjustment to a new academic discipline.

(6) Further reasons for my choice

㉕ I strongly believe that the PhD program in Chemical Engineering will be an ideal venue for me to add expertise in the chemical aspects of fuel cells to my strong background in mechanical engineering. ㉖ I am sure that my mechanical engineering background will offer a different viewpoint because of my specialty in thermal-fluid transport and my theoretical approach to fuel cells. ㉗ The PhD program will ultimately prepare me for a career as an interdisciplinary expert in the field of energy conversion and storage systems. (591 words)

Scene, a meeting between Gene (originally from China) and a writing tutor (Kay):

Gene: Hi, Kay. I emailed you my SOP a couple of days ago. Did you get it, and what do you think?

Kay: Hi, Gene. Yes, I got it, thanks. Did it take you a long time to do it?

Gene: Oh, forever. I think this is my fourth version.

1. Do you think Gene is exaggerating? Does it look like a fourth draft to you?

Kay: Well, my main impression is that you come across as very professional. It seems very very business-like. To me, as an outsider to the field, you make a good case for the need to combine the two engineering fields. I like the detail in paragraph four, and in paragraph five bringing in the names of the professors, and in the middle of the last paragraph hinting at what you can bring to strengthen the program. A great move, Gene! It is also just under the 600-word limit.

2. Do you agree with Kay that these are the strengths of this SOP? Or is she just being nice?

Gene: So far, so good then. But where can I strengthen it?

Kay: Well, what are your own thoughts about that?

Gene: As you know, I am Chinese and I focused on my academic career, past, present, and future. I think other students might include some story, or say something more personal to make the SOP somehow more alive. Another thing. I say nothing about CO_2 emissions from cars, and pollution. This is going to be very bad in my country, China, unless we develop fuel cells for automobiles. Maybe I missed a chance here.

3. Gene makes two main points. Should he include a story? And should he add the part about pollution?

Kay: I don't know if you actually need a story, Gene, but it could be a bit more personal somehow. And bringing in the real world importance of this research seems like an excellent idea.

Gene: Okay. So what do I cut?

4. Simplify Paragraph 3? Leave out the professors in Paragraph 5? Revise Paragraph 1? Your thoughts?

Kay: The first two sentences look rather standard to me. Also, they would seem pretty obvious to your readers, who will be professors in Engineering. That's one place to rethink.

Gene: Fine, thanks. Any other suggestions?

Kay: Well, you might like to have a look at the section in the new textbook by Swales and Feak on Statements of Purpose or Personal Statements, and see what they have to say.

5. Is this a good idea?

Task Five

Either rewrite Gene's opening paragraph to make it more memorable or draft an SOP of your own, whichever is more appropriate for your current circumstances.

Personal Statements

Now consider the case where you have to write two statements, one an SOP similar to Gene's, the other a more definite personal statement. One of the programs at the University of Michigan that requires both is the joint PhD in English and Education. Here is the PS from a successful applicant to this program. As you read it, think about the ways Carl's statement is different from Gene's.

Task Six

Read the Personal Statement, and answer the questions that follow. We have underlined some less common words and phrases, which we discuss in Question 1.

Carl Landrum

Joint PhD Program in English and Education

① My life, compared to the overwhelming majority of people's lives throughout the world, has been one of immense comfort and privilege. ② Growing up white and male in middle class America has afforded me opportunities largely unavailable to the great majority of the world's population. ③ With a respectable (but not unexpected or extraordinary) amount of work, I was easily able to graduate from two world-renowned universities and then obtain a teaching position at one of the top universities in South Korea. ④ In recent years, largely through my living and teaching outside the United States, I have come to realize that privileges such as my own should not be overlooked or taken for granted. ⑤ In my view, people who have had the luxury to encounter few obstacles in their lives and to thereby, through no special effort, gain positions of power have a responsibility to use whatever particular set of interests, talents, and capacities they have been endowed with to decrease the obstacles faced by people in less privileged positions than their own.

⑥ Given my own particular set of interests, talents, and capacities, I would like to contribute toward reversing the many inequalities that I have perceived in the sphere of education. ⑦ I am animated by John Dewey's (1964) observation that "education is the fundamental method of social progress and reform," but at the same time I have found myself increasingly concerned by many educational trends at work in the United States right now. ⑧ In my view, the schooling system in this country is failing to equip the majority of students with the critical confidence and linguistic and rhetorical control—the critical language awareness—needed to develop means of what Chomsky has called "intellectual self-defense" (1999). ⑨ The majority of students are not receiving the language arts training necessary to engage in the type of critical discourse analysis needed for understanding how their societies operate, for identifying patterns of social injustice and methods of coercion employed by institutions of power. ⑩ Nor are students learning the linguistic and rhetorical skills necessary for taking action, for engaging meaningfully in social discourses themselves. ⑪ The spaces where I believe I can contribute toward alleviating these difficult problems are at the interstices between linguistics, English, and education. ⑫ On a very general level, it is in the helping of real students where I have found the drive to work toward a PhD, for I am convinced that research in the fields of English and Education, however theoretical or technical it may be, can and should be relevant to our practical tasks as teachers.

1. We have underlined five words or phrases that may present difficulty. Which of the following offers the correct explanation of their meaning?

   a. they have been endowed with: i. they have acquired; ii. they have inherited

   b. animated: i. influenced; ii. remain enthusiastic about

   c. methods of coercion: i. methods of imprisonment; ii. methods of strong control

   d. alleviating: i. reducing; ii. solving

   e. interstices: i. gaps; ii. places where they meet and connect

2. Would you characterize this text as:

   a. a philosophy of life

   b. a plan for the future

   c. a personal journey

3. In his statement, Carl stresses his social responsibility, primarily by:

   a. stressing his life of privilege

   b. focusing on his international experience

   c. arguing that with privilege comes responsibility

4. Carl supports his educational commitment, primarily by

   a. attacking the educational establishment

   b. showing how theoretical work needs to be made relevant to teaching practice

   c. arguing how underprepared today's undergraduates are for the real world

5. In your view, as an applicant Carl comes across as:

   a. a serious academic intellectual

   b. a person who just wants to settle back in the U.S.

   c. a socially committed educationalist

So, overall, remember that the main difference between the SOP and the PS is that the former tends to focus on what the applicant has done and then plans to do, while the latter focuses on personal thoughts, feelings, and reflections.

Finding Your Voice in the Academic Community

The next four sub-sections assume that you are now attending graduate school. This section deals with some of the essential email interactions that maintain interpersonal contacts within academic settings. (The importance of these types of emails is evidenced in the questionnaire findings from Task One.)

Communicating with Advisors and Committee Members

As an individual academic writer, you will often need to keep others "in the loop" with regard to the progress of your manuscripts (or lack of it!). Instructors (and later editors) may need to know where you stand with regard to upcoming deadlines. Advisors, supervisors, and committee members of master's theses or PhD dissertations (we use the U.S. terminology) also need to know about your progress, especially in these days of increasing pressures in many countries for the timely completion of higher degrees.

Task Seven

With this in mind, here is a draft email message that a graduate student, Akiko, plans to send to her advisor, Caroline Kelly. The email relates to the first version of the second chapter of her dissertation. The student shows the draft of this email message to the three other members of her study group for comments because she is worried that she may not be making a good impression. Their comments follow. Whom do you agree with and why?

Dear Professor Kelly,

I have finally gotten around to writing something. I will put a hard copy in your mailbox sometime next week. Please pick it up and let me know what you think. I hope you like it ☺.

Akiko

Oral Comments:

Leila: "This is short and sweet, Akiko. Although it is a bit vague, I think it will work."

Simon: "I have problems with this, Akiko. Why stress your slowness in the first sentence, and why not specify what exactly you have written? 'Next week' is too vague; how does Professor Kelly know when to look for it? And why don't you say something of what you like and what you don't like about your text, so your advisor is given some direction as to what to focus on? Further, this isn't the time for emoticons! And don't you know your advisor well enough to address her by first name? Please get rid of this draft, and start again."

Isao: As a fellow Japanese, I can see why you wrote such a modest and self-effacing draft, but I am afraid you are not going to make a very good impression on your advisor. I'm afraid that Simon is mostly right.

Now consider how you might revise Akiko's email for her. Before actually writing it, however, consider this email message from a student in Nursing close to finishing her dissertation. She is writing to Frank, the outside member of her committee; Dick and Deb are the co-chairs.

April 12

Hi Frank

   Dick and Deb are reviewing the entire manuscript this week. I am attaching here all seven draft chapters.

   I am certain after talking with Deb & Dick that I will need to do some revising. When we talked, they were satisfied that I understood the points that should be included (particularly regarding the role of gender in nursing practice), but I don't think that I've totally captured this on the printed page.

   I will be at the research group meeting at 4 on Monday April 20. I will be seeing you then, but if you would like to meet before or after regarding any concerns or suggestions you might have, please let me know.

Thanks!

Laura

P.S. In Chapter 4, I decided to go back to the traditional terminology; I hope that is okay. Also, not sure about Chapter 6—too much data and not enough interpretation or explanation?

Some observations on Laura's message:

- Note how Laura "hints" at what Frank might focus on (the role of gender, her use of terminology in Chapter 4, and the possible lack of interpretation in Chapter 6). Frank is being guided here, but indirectly.
- The style of the message is friendly and informal, but also polite. The professors are referred to by their first names, and there are several contractions. As for politeness, notice the way that Laura makes a suggestion in the third paragraph.
- There is enough detail here, but not too much; for example, she refers to her discussion with her co-chairs but only focuses on changes that may be made.

Now offer Akiko an improved draft of her email to her advisor.

Communicating with Co-Authors

In the cases of Akiko and Laura, who are working on their dissertations, we have academic writers primarily responsible for their individual manuscripts. Alternatively, there may be several authors of a manuscript, and often not all of them will necessarily be located in the same place. It is not surprising then that such group writing projects, whether writing for a group term paper or a group master's project, or co-authoring a research paper for publication, can sometimes give rise to confusion and even lead to conflict. In fact, one of our colleagues, Elizabeth Axelson, in her own 2003 dissertation showed how easily this could happen with a multinational group writing a joint master's project in environmental studies. This is another situation then where it can be important to keep everybody "in the loop." Although such networking can be time consuming, it is usually worth the effort in the long run.

Here is a situation that is not unusual. John and Chris are drafting another new small textbook for this series. They are meeting about the project. At the meeting, they are joined again by Vera, their regular research assistant, and Emma, an English major just starting an internship on the project. John has sent an attachment containing the material he has been working on. Unfortunately, and by mistake, he circulated an earlier draft for comments. (This is not the first time he has done this.) He receives two email messages, one from his long-standing co-author and colleague and one from Emma.

Message 1

Hi, John,

I have just wasted a couple of hours writing comments on your draft section on describing procedures in Methods sections, only to discover that the text I have been working on is NOT the latest version. Can you please make sure to put the date of the draft at the top every time you modify it? Otherwise, everything gets confused. Thanks.

Chris

Message 2

Professor Swales,

I have been looking at your draft attachment, and I am just beginning to wonder whether I am looking at your latest version. For one thing, I seem to remember from last week's meeting that you planned to change Task Six. Before I start working on this, would it be possible for you to check that I have the correct version? By the way, I am very excited to be working on this project. Thanks for choosing me!

Emma

As you can see, these two emails on the same topic are very different in style. And this is largely determined by the relationship between the sender and the receiver. What differences do you notice?

Task Eight

Now suppose you are Vera, who has worked with John and Chris on a part-time basis for more than a year and who now has her PhD and who also works as a lecturer in Russian and German. Write her email on the same topic to John Swales. It should, of course, be somewhere between the other two in terms of style and politeness.

As the previous activity implies, the smooth management of group writing tasks can be a complex matter, and often unexpected difficulties can arise (as with John sending the wrong attachment). And it is not yet clear whether new technologies such as Google Docs or other file-sharing programs can regularly solve the problems that arise.

Obviously, it is better to establish certain "ground rules" somewhere toward the beginning of joint projects. The following task is designed to help you focus on some possible ground rules.

Task Nine

Here are a number of suggestions of various kinds for managing group writing tasks. Evaluate them in terms of their importance, and then undertake the writing task. (Not all of them will necessarily be "very important.")

V = very important
S = somewhat important
N = not really important

_____ 1. During the work on the project, establish who will be busiest with other commitments and who will be least busy.

_____ 2. Everybody should agree to date all the drafts at the top, so that members don't respond to out-of-date texts.

_____ 3. The order of authors on the final manuscript should be decided at the beginning.

_____ 4. Agree early on formatting issues, such as choice of font and font size.

_____ 5. Work out a clear and realistic timetable for completing the project on time.

_____ 6. Make contingency plans in case something goes wrong (e.g., illness in a group member's immediate family).

_____ 7. Try to decide who might be best at what (e.g., literature review, data collection, statistics, stylistic elegance, etc.).

_____ 8. Do not penalize non-native speakers by restricting them to tasks that do not require writing or participation in an oral presentation (e.g., doing the statistical analysis, making tables and charts).

For 9 and 10, write two recommendations of your own, and evaluate them.

_____ 9. _____

_____ 10. _____

Now take one of the suggestions you ranked as *very important*, and write a suitable message to your (imaginary) co-authors, indicating how the suggestion could best be implemented.

Requests and Reminders

Earlier you saw a message from Chris to John asking him to make sure he dates his manuscript drafts. Since they know each other well, this kind of request is straightforward. However, if your message is a first-time, unexpected communication addressed to somebody you don't know—someone even in another country—the situation can become more delicate. And here we might indeed reflect on the part of the Introductory Section that dealt with the placement of the request; "out of the blue" requests may need some prior explanation before making the actual request.

Consider this situation: You are a research assistant for Dr. Walter Lee in the Centre for Management Studies at one of the Hong Kong universities. At Dr. Lee's instruction, you send this email message:

Dear Dr. Rogers,

I am a research assistant for Dr. Walter Lee, whose work you may be familiar with. We have recently read with considerable interest your recent article in *Management Science* on politeness strategies in call centers. We note that you cite an unpublished working paper on the same topic. We were wondering whether it be possible for you to send us an electronic version of this paper? We believe it will help us in our own research.

With best wishes

Emily Chang (research assistant)

As you can see, this request message is both polite and professional. Also note that Emily (correctly) gives her full name at the end of the message. It is particularly important to do this if your email name is different from your real name or your real name isn't part of your email address (such as happygal@ or compoman@). Adding your position can be useful too.

Despite having sent a polite and professional email message, Emily has received no response after two weeks.

Task Ten

Which of these next steps do you prefer—and why?

1. Resend the original message again.

2. Send this message as a test.

   Dr. Rogers, did you get my email of June 12 regarding a request for one of your papers? I am beginning to wonder whether it got trapped in your spam box, or perhaps you have been out of email contact?

3. Explain to Professor Lee that you have had no reply, and suggest that it might work better if he sent a message personally.

4. Resend the message, adding the following:

   In the meantime, I am attaching a working paper on a similar topic that might be of interest to you.

Language Focus: The "Attitudinal" or Polite Past

There is a small set of words and phrases that can occur in or with a past tense, but with present meaning. Consider this email:

> Hi Professor Jones. *I just wanted* to let you know that I got the fellowship I applied for. Thanks for all your help.

The writer here has chosen the attitudinal past in order to send a polite, if informal, communication to the professor. Compare this with the real past:

> Hi Professor Jones. *I really wanted* to see the movie you recommended, but by the time I found a free evening it was no longer being shown in town.

Or this example:

Attitudinal (hope still alive):

> Professor Jones, I was hoping that we could meet sometime next week.

Real (hope denied):

> Professor Jones, I was hoping to meet you in office hours next week, but now I have to leave town because of illness in my family.

In many cases, the attitudinal past not only expresses politeness, but also deference and distance. For example, you hear that your boss urgently wants to see you on some matter. Rather than popping your head around her door and saying, "You wanna see me?" you might more nervously offer: "Did you want to see me?"

However, the phrases that can take the attitudinal past are very limited.

curious   I was just curious about your views on this.

wanted   The two other things I just wanted to mention are firstly . . .

wondering   I was just wondering if you have had a chance to look at the draft.

thinking   I was thinking we might finish early today.

hoping   I was hoping we might meet later this week.

As these examples show, the attitudinal past seems to be restricted to polite inquiries and questions as well as to expressions of wishes, thoughts, and hopes. Also notice that the first three of the examples are hedged with **just,** which makes them even more polite and tentative. **Just** is common with these phrases and is typically pronounced as [ĵəs].

Finally, notice that in her email message Emily Chang uses the attitudinal past when she very politely writes:

We were wondering whether it would be possible . . .

Now would be a good time to check your own messages (as well as some incoming ones) to look for instances of the attitudinal past. (And also check the student's language in the cartoon on page 1.)

Task Eleven

You (and your partner) are assistants to Professor Gardener. He forwards you these five email request messages on pages 30–33, accompanied by this one from him.

> Guys, these requests just in. They never seem to stop. What should be our priorities here? Could you sort them out in rank order, with either the most urgent, or those easiest to comply with, at the top (i.e., 1)? Then at the weekly lab meeting we can decide what to do—or not to do! Thanks for doing this for me.

Read the messages, and complete the chart on page 33. Then sort the requests as per Professor Gardener's instructions. What are your reasons for your choices? What do you think the decisions will be at next week's lab meeting?

(To save space, we have sometimes left out email addresses, subject lines, mailing addresses, etc., in the messages.)

Message 1

From: martino@unimolf.it
To: Gardener@xxx.edu
Subject: Request

Dear Sir,

I am a researcher at a small local university here near Palermo, and am carrying out research in your area of materials science. I would like to visit your department as an observer researcher for a short time (about three months) in order to get ideas about my thesis.

As I am a native speaker of Italian, I would be delighted to help your students learn Italian in your modern languages department, or I could collaborate in any other way that you can suggest.

If you accept, I could come during the next academic term. Please let me know your answer as soon as possible since I need to apply for a travel grant. Looking forward to hearing from you.

Yours faithfully,

Message 2

Dear Professor,

I am currently working on a master's thesis on the processes of metallic-ceramic fusion, and I have recently read a recent and highly relevant paper by your group in *Materials Science Digest* (2010, Vol. 45, pp. 345–357). I was wondering if there are similar papers on this topic that you could refer me to or let me have copies of? (The library here isn't very good.)

My advisor here is Ana Augusto, who sends her regards. She met you at the Caracas conference in 2008.

Rosinda de Souza

Rua Campo Verde, 174–apto. 12

Bela Colina–MG

CEP 12340-187

Brasil

Message 3

Dear Professor Gardener,

First let me introduce myself. I have recently returned to Malaysia, having completed a PhD at Desert University with Dr. William D. Jones as advisor, who has recently retired. On return, I was asked to start a small research group on materials science in our research institute. On Dr. Jones's suggestion, I am asking whether you might be willing to act as an informal and unofficial advisor to my group. I know you are a very busy and important man, but if you happened to be in this part of the world (we know you sometimes go to Australia), my colleagues and I would greatly appreciate a visit of a few days or so. Unfortunately, we have no funds for international travel, but we can cover regional travel and all local expenses.

Dr. Ali Osman

Materials Science Research Group

Sarawak Science Research Institute

Message 4

Dear Professor Gardener,

This is a preliminary inquiry as to whether you might be in principle willing to act as external examiner for a PhD thesis from here on metallic-ceramic fusion. The thesis is expected to be completed next month, and the defense will need to take place within two months of the submission date. We would expect a two- to three-page evaluation. There is no need for you to be present in Hong Kong for the defense itself. The university is able to pay a small fee for this important service. If you would like any further information, please do not hesitate to ask.

If you would be able to accept (and I can imagine how busy you must be), I will forward your name to the central administration, which will then take up the administrative details.

With best wishes,

Henry Liu

Head, Department of Materials Science

Shatin University

Hong Kong

Message 5

Dear Professor Gardener,

I am writing to you on the recommendation of Professor Grossman here in Vienna, where I am his research assistant and working part-time on my dissertation, which has the provisional title "Ceramic-Metallic Fusion Properties at Extremely High Temperatures." I understand from Professor Grossman that you have done a lot of work in this area. Since I would certainly like to base my work on the latest results and methods, I really need your help! I am especially interested in your publications, latest experiments and their results. I would also be grateful if you have any suggestions about my dissertation topic and for any further bibliographic references that would aid me in my research. I thank you very much in advance and only hope that it won't require too much of an effort for you to help me. Looking forward to hearing from you soon!

Yours sincerely,

Annika Graf

	Message 1	Message 2	Message 3	Message 4	Message 5
Academic status of requester					
Type of help requested					
Place in text where main request occurs (beginning, middle, or end?)					
Phrases you like					
Phrases you dislike					
Rank order					

In our considerable experience with using this task in classes and workshops, most people choose Message 4 as being the most urgent; Professor Liu really needs to know whether Professor Gardener can act as examiner. Most people also give the lowest priority to Message 5, principally because it asks for too much.

Task Twelve

Offer Annika Graf a revised version of her request message.

> ### Language Focus: *to* + VERB+*ing* Patterns
>
> You may have noticed that two of the requests use the common closing phrase: **looking forward _to hearing_ from you.** This is perhaps the classic instance of this verb pattern. Other phrases are useful for other kinds of writing, such as recommendations, reports, and research papers.
>
> For many non-native speakers of English this pattern is counterintuitive since they have been typically taught in schools that verbs can be followed by either another infinitive (**She hopes to improve**) or a participial form (**She hates revising**). **To** + VERB+**ing** seems to break these well-known rules. This structure, however, can occur after a number of grammatical items.
>
> A. **To** + VERB+**ing** following certain verbs; here are some of the more common ones:
>
> I am **looking forward to receiving** further information.
>
> He is **committed to teaching** all kinds of students.
>
> Her experience is not **limited to teaching** in the United States.
>
> She is **used to running** complex statistical tests.
>
> She **objected to having** to redo the assignment.
>
> They **admitted to failing** to follow the safety procedures.

B. **To** + VERB+**ing** following some complex prepositions:

In addition to working on his dissertation, he is also teaching a class.

Prior to entering the PhD program, she worked in industry.

With a view to increasing enrollment, the department has developed an interactive website.

C. **To** + VERB+**ing** following certain adjectives:

She is **close to completing** her latest project.

This **is crucial to understanding** the nature of the problem.

The director may be **open to rescheduling** the meeting.

He is not **resistant to being** relocated.

D. **To** + VERB+**ing** following certain nouns:

There was no **alternative to repeating** the experiment.

She has several **objections to being** labeled a "radical feminist."

His **approach to understanding** society is more psychological than sociological.

There was considerable **resistance to implementing** the curricular reform.

Task Thirteen

I. Complete these sentences with an appropriate VERB+*ing*.

1. I am looking forward to _____ your presentation at next month's conference.

2. The director is not accustomed to _____ his decisions questioned.

3. The student admitted to _____ the term paper from the Internet.

4. The tax reform is being introduced with a view toward _____ benefits for the poor.

5. There can be drawbacks to _____ on probabilistic measures.

6. She is averse to _____ her dissertation abstract for a sixth time.

II. Look through some of your emails and other texts to check on your use of this hard-to-learn syntactic pattern. For example, check on your use of the word *alternative* to see whether you write:

One alternative *to repeat* the study is. . . .

Or the correct:

One alternative *to repeating* the study is. . . .

Writing Apologies

Written apologies these days are much more likely to be made by email rather than in the form of a letter. Apologies can, of course, vary greatly in formality and length depending on (a) the relationship between the correspondents and (b) the topic of the apology. For space reasons, we will focus only on apologies for delay in responding—a common situation for many of us.

Task Fourteen

Here are six email messages to John. Mark them as FF (very formal), F (formal), I (informal), or II (very informal). Also, can you guess the relationship of the sender to the receiver (in this case, John)? Work in pairs if possible.

_____ 1. Hi John. Excuse the long silence. Been so busy running around that I'm hardly ever in my office. Anyway, I'm attaching what I think you want. Lemme know if it isn't okay. Best.

_____ 2. I apologize for being slow to respond to your request for information. This was reviewed by the board at its last meeting. However, the discussion was highly complex and it was, after the meeting, difficult to discern the actual instructions for how to respond to you. Further conversations with the chair now allow me to say . . .

_____ 3. Dear John. Forgive the delay, caused in the first instance by a faulty fax machine, from which it was difficult to extract your message. Then, we had trouble getting the machine to work properly. However, the delay does not signify a lack of interest in your suggestion. Warm regards.

_____ 4. John, I am sorry to have taken so long to get back to you on this. With my new job I've been literally run off my feet. Might I suggest we get together for lunch one day? Perhaps if you could suggest two or three days that work for you before the end of the month, then Keith and I can select one and firm up arrangements.

_____ 5. Professor Swales, we apologize for being slow to getting you payment for your recent work for us as an external examiner. This was caused by an oversight in the accounting office, which has now been rectified. Sincerely.

_____ 6. Groveling apologies for being so slow. Recently, I have been running into a whole heap of technical problems, including a dreadful computer crash. Anyway, finally here is what you wanted.

All six apologies give some kind of explanation for the delay.

Are the explanations convincing to you?
Would you expect something more?

Language Focus: *Run* as a Phrasal Verb

In Task Fourteen, three of the apologies used **run** as a phrasal verb, as in **run around, run off** (my feet), and **run into**. You may have noticed that **run** as a phrasal verb occurs in the more informal messages. Phrasal **run** is widely used in informal speech and writing. Here are five examples of the phrasal verbs featuring **run** that you may find useful:

   a. I **ran across** Bill the other day—I haven't seen him for ages! He reminded me that I owed you a response.

   b. Apologies for missing the meeting. Stupidly, I **ran out of** gas on the highway.

   c. The battery in my laptop is really **run down**. I had better sign off. Sorry.

   d. Hi! Alas, a family issue has come up, and I am not going to make the meeting tomorrow when we are supposed to **run through** the results so far.

   e. I don't want to **run away from** my responsibilities here, but one of my children is ill and I won't be able to complete my part of the project by Friday. Apologies to you all. I hope to catch up next week.

Establishing Yourself in Graduate School

This section addresses four supporting written genres—that is, types of text that are not in public view (unlike, say, published book reviews). The first three are all types of applications of various kinds and, thus, typically play an important part in junior scholars' lives as they try to find the support they need in order to fulfill their academic and research aspirations. The fourth and final one is very different since it deals with letters of recommendation. Initially, it might be thought that graduate students would not be writing these types of letters, but more likely to be requesting that they be written on their behalf. However, in our experience, graduate students are often asked to write letters for undergraduates they have taught or to write letters about their instructors who are coming up for tenure, or promotion.

Small Grant Applications

Internal departmental and research group applications for small amounts of funding are usually handled quickly and informally without a great deal of paper work. So far, so good then. However, more competitive ones may require some written explanation and justification.

Task Fifteen

At some point you may want or need to apply for a small grant—perhaps to make a research trip of some kind, or for some equipment, or to attend a conference. Often these grants are competitive, and so you need to make the best case you can for getting the money.

You (and your partner, if you have one) are members of the selection committee for a university-wide competition for summer research grants, with a maximum level of support of $2,000. The extracts from two applications from very different fields follow. Both fall within the budget limit. Read the applications, and decide which of the arguments from your fellow committee members you agree with.

A. This first is from the Department of Modern Languages.

Brief Project Description

My dissertation work focuses in part on an important but little-known thirteenth century Spanish encyclopedia called *Lucidario*. There is a low-quality edition of this work published in 1968 and seven mediaeval manuscripts, which can be found in Madrid and Salamanca. I am currently working with this unsatisfactory 1968 edition, and I believe that reading the original manuscripts will greatly deepen our understanding of this work. This is because the manuscripts vary in their treatment of certain central issues, such as their use of Aristotle and the inclusion and role of fictional characters. Studying these original sources will throw new light on the significance of the *Lucidario*, particularly with regard to its relationship to intellectual trends of the late thirteenth century.

I am therefore requesting funds for a two-month research trip to Spain to study the seven manuscripts. A detailed budget estimate is given on the following page.

Ana Martinez (doctoral pre-candidate)

B. The second comes from another pre-candidate, this time from the School of Architecture.

Brief Project Description

I would like to request summer support for my ongoing research project on new types of load-bearing composite panels for use in wall systems. This research is valuable since it concerns innovative sustainable building materials, which may well reduce energy and material building costs in the building industry. Since this project involves laboratory testing and computer simulation, it is necessary to construct specimen testing materials. Therefore my request consists of funds to:

1. Purchase the materials for making sustainable composite panels for testing;

2. Employ a technician to modify the current equipment for testing this type of panel.

Although my advisor and I are assured of funds to continue this research starting in the coming fall, this summer support is needed so that momentum can be maintained and I can obtain candidacy before the next academic year. Thank you for your consideration. A detailed budget estimate is attached.

Regards,

Esmail Najdi

Arguments in committee

Mark the points with which you agree with an A (agree) and those with which you disagree with a D (disagree).

Ana's Application

_____ 1. Ana doesn't show any effort to obtain alternative funds. Also, what does *focuses in part* mean? I don't know, as a result, whether this trip to Spain is crucial for her dissertation or not. I'm inclined to turn this one down.

_____ 2. We all know that the Modern Languages Department never has any real discretionary money, and Ana's project is so specialized that it is unlikely that anybody else in the U would fund it. I also read the *focuses in part* phrase differently; to me it suggests that she will be offering the field more than a narrow archive-based textual study. I vote to give her the money.

_____ 3. Look guys, I may be an engineer and all that, but I don't see much value in this kind of historical scholarship. Surely, we should be supporting projects that are more relevant to life in our century, not the thirteenth. For me, it's "no."

_____ 4. We are a major research university with a serious commitment to scholarship in many forms. Ana's project looks outward to Spain at a very interesting time in its history, because it is through Islamic Spain that Aristotle was rediscovered in Europe. Unlike my engineering colleague, I think it is well worth considering.

Esmail's Application

_____ 1. It looks as though these guys in Architecture messed up their funding support, and are asking us to get them out of a hole. Since *sustainability* is such a buzzword these days, they should have been able to do better. I don't think we should be providing such bridge funds when we have so many other strong applications to consider.

_____ 2. It seems to me, on the contrary, that one of the prime purposes of the summer research grants system is precisely to provide the kind of funds that Esmail is requesting. Our sums are small and in this case, they will go far. I recommend that we approve this funding.

_____ 3. The project description is a little vague, but if you look at the detailed budget, it becomes much clearer what kinds of material are needed and in what quantities. Some of these are really experimental and cannot be easily fabricated on-site. Given this, and the potential industrial applications of this research, I vote for "yes."

_____ 4. As an engineer, I am concerned that the first priority should be that the testing equipment works. There is no point in purchasing relatively expensive materials until we are assured that the testing and simulation programs are running smoothly. Although I was initially impressed with this project, now I have concerns about its viability. So, reluctantly, it's a "no" from me.

Any other considerations you would like to enter into the discussion of these two candidates? Any advice for strengthening the Brief Project Descriptions (within the 150 word limit)?

Letters for Teaching/Research Assistant/ Student Assistant Positions

As with applications the allocation of teaching assistant (TA) positions within a department is usually undertaken seriously but fairly informally, while short-term, part-time research assistants (RA) positions are usually assigned by the senior researcher in charge. However, if it is necessary to look outside, then a request for applications will probably need to be posted.

Our own home base, the English Language Institute at the University of Michigan, does not have its own graduate students, so we need to look elsewhere. Imagine this scenario: We are looking for a doctoral student to work part-time as a graduate student research assistant (GSRA) for two months to help with a project examining the strengths and weaknesses of international students as dissertation writers. We post an email message asking for a short expression of interest to be accompanied by a CV (see pages 85–91).

We get a number of responses.

Task Sixteen

Rank these four email responses, with 1 being the best. First, read the discussion points on page 45. Which two applicants would you interview, and why?

Applicant A

I would like to apply for the GSRA position offered by ELI for next spring term—"Examining the strengths and weaknesses of international students as dissertation writers." I am a senior graduate student in physics and currently preparing for writing my PhD thesis. I am applying for this position because I need financial assistance in completing my PhD dissertation. Also, I think the research project will help my dissertation writing by observing other people's weaknesses. As an international student, I am also having a problem in writing. Thus, I can better understand than native speakers what are the hidden weak points of international students' writing. As a physics student, I am quite familiar with the statistical analysis of data; so hopefully I can provide new insights into the data. I am afraid you may think that language students are more suitable for this job; however, if you are going to research writing in science, I am sure I can be helpful. My CV is attached. I am looking forward to your reply.

Applicant B

Regarding the duties of this GSRA position, an outstanding knowledge of statistical computer packages and good English communication skills are necessary. I used to be a computer laboratory assistant and am also a teaching assistant for experiment design and statistics computer programs. I do therefore believe my experience can meet the needs of this position. My curriculum vitae is attached as an appendix. If you have further questions, please do not hesitate to contact me. Thank you!

Applicant C

I am writing to express my interest in the GSRA position for the Spring term in your department. I am currently completing my dissertation under the direction of Dr. _____ and Dr._____ . I am expecting to fulfill all the PhD requirements by the end of this year. Enclosed please find my current vita that expounds upon my academic experiences and particular areas of research interest. Through years of training, I have developed several skills in statistical and quantitative analyses, especially in the areas of sampling and questionnaire analysis. With this knowledge and experience I have, I am confident that I can make a significant contribution to your project. I would be glad to schedule a meeting with you at your convenience. Thank you for your consideration. I look forward to hearing from you.

Applicant D

Dissertation writing, for most graduate students, is an important part of their study. But for international students, besides specific rules, structures, and formats, cultural differences can bring up more difficulties. To discover the strengths and weaknesses of dissertation writers, several experiments can be conducted, among them, analyzing questionnaire results, interviewing with students and faculty, and tabulating the interview data. For the last four years, I have been an international graduate student in the Department of Electrical Engineering and Computer Science. My excellent communication skills have enabled me to reach candidacy, my training has given me strong analytic skills; above all as an Asian, my cultural background will reflect the distinct problems that most international students will encounter in their dissertation writing. Therefore, I am the right candidate for this GSRA position. I attach my CV as requested.

Discussion Points

Imagine you are the faculty member deciding who to hire. Consider:

1. Do you have any concerns about any of the applicants' written English?

2. How important do you think statistical skills will be?

3. Should you be looking for signs of cross-cultural sensitivity?

4. Should you pay any attention to apparent student need, or focus only on who would be best for the ELI?

5. If Applicant B asks you for suggestions about how to improve the posted message, what advice would you give?

Fellowship Applications

Today, a wide range of scholarships, fellowships, and grants are available for junior scholars and researchers in the United States. Often the application instructions are quite specific and thus helpful with regard to what should and should not be included in the application. It therefore pays to carefully read the guidelines given. For example, if the instructions state that application letters should be no longer than two double-spaced pages, do not write half a page or three single-spaced pages. Look at this fellowship announcement, and then do Task Seventeen.

Applications are invited for Miller Fellowships 201X–201X

Miller Fellowships are available each year to support Asian female graduate students from Turkey to Japan to facilitate field research in Asia. The scholarships award up to a full six months' support including travel, living expenses, health insurance, and related research expenses. We expect to offer four scholarships for the coming year.

Applicants should provide a recent CV, the names of two referees, transcripts, and proof of Asian nationality (such as a photocopy of a valid passport). Applications should also be accompanied by a statement of purpose of no more than 250 words explaining how a Miller Fellowship would contribute to the applicant's further academic development. In this statement applicants must also clearly indicate how their work will further the position of Asian women in their country upon their return home. Applications are due in the Miller Scholarship Offices by November 15. Awards will be announced on December 20.

Task Seventeen

Your acquaintance from Korea, Ji-Young Kim, is looking for financial support to conduct her field research back home. She has written three versions of her statement of purpose for the Miller Fellowship so far, and each time she has received feedback via email from her advisor. She is now a bit confused and needs your advice as to which one to submit and then whether the best of the set needs further work. Read through her drafts (and commentaries) and then decide which would likely be the most successful. What are the strong and weak points of each? Then send an email to Ji-Young giving your considered opinion. In this case, we have added sentence numbers because we have included some *Language Notes* at the end of the three versions.

Version A

① My name is Ji-Young Kim and I am a beginning second-year female master's student of Korean nationality in the School of Social Work. ② As you can see from my transcript, my grades for my first year's coursework are very encouraging. ③ This year I really need a Miller Fellowship so that I can go back to Korea to collect data for my thesis. ④ My main area of interest is in gerontology, particularly in long term care provisions for elderly widows. ⑤ I could base my thesis on United States data and experiences, but both my advisor and I think it would be more useful for me to collect Korean data, especially since this issue has been little addressed by Korean social work researchers. ⑥ My own family experience demonstrates how real the problem is. ⑦ I have two elderly aunts (both now in their 80s and widowed) who live in rural areas quite a long way from their relatives and who are virtual "shut-ins." ⑧ They are visited by an untrained church volunteer only once a week, and by their families only once or twice a year. ⑨ As demonstrated by my aunts, this is a serious problem, and when I return to Korea I would like to be able to do more for them and for other elderly women in similar situations. ⑩ This is why a Miller Fellowship is very important for my future.

Commentary

Not bad, Ji-Young. I think you explain your need for the fellowship quite well—indeed you might overdo it a bit. However, the main problem is that the selection committee will likely conclude that you haven't thought through what data you will need and how you are going to collect it. Please try again, and try to write a bit more formally. Susan

Version B

① As can be seen from my supporting documentation, I am beginning my second year in the master's program in social work. ② I plan to complete my degree in July 201X after I have written and defended my master's thesis. ③ My primary professional interest is in the interface between social work and gerontology, more specifically in the care of elderly women whose husbands have died and who are not cared for by their family members. ④ Recent demographic data show that this at-risk group is growing rapidly in many parts of the world, including Korea. ⑤ My advisor, Dr. Susan Grant, has suggested that, since I plan to return to Korea on completing my degree, it would be advantageous if I could base my thesis on Korean data. ⑥ Unfortunately, little information is available in this country, which is why I am applying for a Miller Fellowship. ⑦ If I am successful, I plan to spend three months in Korea in my hometown of Kunsan. ⑧ There I will interview a stratified sample of 40 elderly widows in order to develop a profile of how well the municipality is coping with this growing problem. ⑨ Without a Miller Fellowship I will not be able to carry out my plan. ⑩ Thank you for your consideration.

Commentary

Well done, Ji-Young. This is much more professional. I like the way you offer a coherent research plan toward the end of your text. But I don't think you should suggest that going to Korea is my idea. And maybe you should put the action research issue first, rather than presenting your personal details? One more go perhaps?

Version C

① Rising life expectancies, especially for women, are creating increasing social problems in many parts of the world. ② The latest available Korean government census data show that 53 percent of Korean women in their 80s are either widowed or have never been married; of these nearly 30 percent are living alone and are rarely visited by their family members. ③ Current Korean social policy toward the elderly is at least partly premised on the traditional Asian concept of filial piety, i.e., that younger family members will take care of their elderly relatives, but as the above statistics show, this tradition is not as strong as it once was. ④ My advisor, Prof. Susan Grant, agrees that an appropriate topic for my upcoming thesis would be an onsite investigation of the medical, financial, and emotional status of elderly widows in my hometown of Kunsan, Korea. ⑤ If this investigation works as planned, Dr. Grant and I plan to submit a joint article comparing United States and Korean approaches to this problem. ⑥ If I am awarded a Miller Fellowship, I plan to carry out the case-study phase of the research from January to April as well as work on preliminary analyses of the findings. ⑦ I would then return to the university to write up my thesis and then hopefully defend in June.

Commentary

Oh, Ji-Young, these applications are so difficult! What you have written is an excellent rationale for your research. However, I am not sure that the latest version will work so well with the selection committee, who might want more of an overt social commitment. Oh dear, let me think some more about this. Best, Susan.

Consult these *Language notes* if you wish.

1. <u>Version A–Sentence 1</u>. There is a natural tendency, especially perhaps among Asian students, to want to introduce themselves at the beginning by name, as Ji-Young does in this instance. This practice tends to surprise American readers; it is not necessary, especially in more formal documents, when the writer's name will appear at the end.

2. <u>Version A–Sentence 2; Version B–Sentence 1</u>. Notice that the passive statement in VB, *As can be seen from my supporting documentation* does not have a subject, although this is a finite clause. It is easy to want to put an *it* in here, but the sentence is, in fact, correctly written. For a fuller discussion of this, see *Academic Writing for Graduate Students,* pp. 122–124.

3. <u>Version A–Sentence 7; Version C–Sentence 3.</u> In S7 Ji-Young has correctly put the colloquial term *shut-ins* in what are called *scare quotes*, presumably to show that she recognizes that this may not be standard academic language. Another phrase that might have been "scare-quoted" is *filial piety* in VC, because it is a special expression. We are only just getting an understanding of how these uses of quotation marks work, but it is clear that established academic writers use them quite a lot even when many writing instructional texts advise against their use (c.f. Aull & Barcy, 2010).

4. <u>Version A–Sentence 5</u>. Note the clever use of *could* in *I could base my thesis on*. This implies it would be possible, but that it is not optimal. Compare these similar conversational uses:
   a. I *could* come in over the weekend, I suppose. (but would rather not)
   b. She *could* refuse the job offer. (it's possible but not in her best interests to do so.)

5. <u>Version C–Sentence 6</u>. Notice Ji-Young has chosen the more direct—and more confident—option here:
   a. If I am awarded . . . , I plan to carry out. . . .

   As opposed to:
   b. If I were to be awarded . . . , I would plan. . . .

6. Version C–Sentence 7. Finally, note the use of *I would then return*. This is a conditional and has nothing to do with the past. It is dependent on the *if* clause at the beginning of S6.

Task Eighteen

Now it's your turn. Write an email message to Ji-Young, explaining your choice of your preferred version.

Letters of Recommendation

At some point in your academic career you will likely be asked to write a letter of recommendation for a student or colleague, such as for undergraduates or more junior graduates you have worked with. Moreover, in the United States, graduate students may be asked to write letters for assistant professors in their department who are being considered for tenure. Letters of recommendation are one of those genres that often bear the stamp of the academic culture in which they were written. For example, American letters tend to be very positive and enthusiastic, whereas British ones tend to be more neutral and more guarded. Such differences can, of course, lead to misunderstandings.

Task Nineteen

Read this letter of recommendation for an undergraduate student applying to a master's program in Public Policy and then respond to the eight reaction statements on page 52.

February 24, 2010

To Whom It May Concern

I am pleased to be writing this letter of recommendation for Kristen Matthews, who was one of my students in fall term 2009. While she was my student she was very hard-working, punctual, and well mannered in class. She worked well with others on projects and always turned in solid work. Her final project was exceptionally well designed and creative. She is very honest, mature, and self-motivated. Her outgoing personality made her a pleasure to have in class.

While assisting Ms. Matthews with her papers during my office hours, I really got to know her quite well. As it turns out, she has an excellent background in public affairs, having spent two summers as an intern with the Democratic party. In this role, she was primarily responsible for encouraging various minorities to vote in elections. Ms. Matthews has also been politically active on campus, being vice-president in the recent presidential campaign. Ms. Matthews would like to pursue a career related to public policy, most likely as a staff member in a municipal social services department, or for a similarly oriented non-profit organization. Given her performance in my class, and her range of extra-curricular activities, I am quite sure she will succeed as she pursues a professional degree in public policy.

Sincerely,

Here are some reactions to this letter. Do you agree or disagree, and why?

1. *This is a nice letter about a nice person by a nice person, but it may not help her too much.*

2. *This is a very nice letter that should work very well.*

3. *There is no need to write* To Whom It May Concern. *It doesn't do any good, and may do harm.*

4. *Why does the writer consistently refer to the applicant as* Ms. Matthews *in the second half of the letter? I would have used her first name.*

5. *The writer doesn't say what course she was teaching. Why not? I am guessing it had nothing to do with politics.*

6. *The formal use of* Ms. Matthews *in the second half suggests that the applicant is a serious, mature individual.*

7. While assisting Ms. Matthews with her papers *gives an impression that the student has a serious writing problem. This needs rephrasing.*

8. *The first paragraph has useful detail; the second does not.*

Language Focus: Positive and Less Positive Language in Letters of Recommendation

Look at this list of adjectives and adverbs. Could any of them perhaps carry negative connotations without the addition of supporting evidence? Place a check mark (✓) next to the adjectives you think an applicant for an academic position (such as yourself) might like to see in a letter of recommendation.

_____ articulate	_____ creative	_____ observant
_____ nice	_____ imaginative	_____ self-confident
_____ dependable	_____ satisfactory	_____ eager
_____ effective	_____ assertive	_____ adequate
_____ pleasant	_____ efficient	_____ cheerful
_____ good	_____ innovative	_____ cooperative
_____ mature	_____ steady	_____ critical

As we have seen in the recommendation letter for Ms. Matthews, a letter that is short on relevant and "winning" details may do very little to help a candidate. After all, more often than not, students in general are described as outstanding, creative, and in the top 20 percent of their class. Thus, in order to distinguish a candidate, it is important to provide examples that demonstrate how a candidate is exemplary or worthy of recognition. Also bear in mind that a vague letter of recommendation—one that is general and lacks specific examples—may be viewed as a relatively weak recommendation, as the reader tries to second-guess why the letter lacks detail. (The writer cannot remember much about the applicant? The writer's experience of the applicant is limited?)

Now notice how this section from a letter of recommendation provides the detail necessary to really support the candidate. The letter was part of an extensive file for a graduate student being (successfully) nominated for the Outstanding Graduate Student Instructor Award. It was written by a senior faculty member very experienced in writing (and reading) such letters.

I can more explicitly address Jasmine's teaching abilities by describing her contributions to our Graduate Student Instructor (GSI) Training course last term. First, I should point out that Jasmine was chosen as the program's Graduate Student Mentor this year based on a combination of her breadth of experience with our courses and her highly regarded teaching style. In the past the GSI training course met for one hour per week, but in our meetings before the term, Jasmine suggested that we instead have four three-hour class meetings in order to facilitate interactions and discussions. Throughout, she had an integral role in the course design and execution, and throughout I was delighted with her creativity. For example, Jasmine organized the videotaping of selected discussion sections from Botany courses being taught for use in the seminar. She then developed role-playing office hours or sample homework exercises around appropriate portions of the videotapes. As a specific instance, in one snippet of videotape from a section of "Introduction to Botany" a bright undergraduate student asked an excellent question about hybridization and the identification problems it creates. The discussion leader followed up briefly, but it was clear that the student was not quite satisfied with the answer. The follow-up role play involved the undergraduate (played by Jasmine or me) coming to an office hour of the discussion leader (played by a seminar student) to mercilessly pursue this point. One of Jasmine's greatest inspirations was to have students take a "multi-headed" approach to role playing. For example, in the office hour just described, rather than put a single student on the spot in the role of discussion leader, Jasmine decided to "freeze frame" the office hour, during which time the target seminar student consulted with the other students before unfreezing the scenario and returning to the office hour attendee. This worked beautifully, not only setting the students at ease, but also stimulating creative, thoughtful solutions.

Would you agree that the explicit details make a big difference?

Task Twenty

What type of support could be offered to justify the following unsupported statements made in various recommendations. Don't just say, *Give examples*. Be creative, and make up examples for at least two of them.

1. Desiree has obtained one of the best grade point averages in our program, and she has done magnificent work in the materials laboratory.

2. Throughout her time as an undergraduate, Maria has been active in extracurricular activities.

3. Sergei is a very responsible person.

4. Mitsuyo is an excellent communicator.

5. Over the years it has become clear that Antonia is a very motivated student who sets high goals for herself.

These days, especially in the United States, it seems letters of recommendation say little that is negative. However, occasionally you may think that it is important to discuss something potentially negative regarding a candidate. For example, you may be concerned that the candidate might not make a good impression when interviewed or has something in his or her background that needs explaining; then you may want to discuss this in the letter and offer some explanation.

Task Twenty-One

Read this short section from the final paragraph of a letter of recommendation written for a graduate student applying for a junior faculty position. Consider the questions that follow.

> Melissa Jones has an abundance of talent, energy, and knowledge. But let me end by confessing to a small anxiety. I have already said that she can sometimes be quiet and shy in more social occasions, although at other times she can be vibrant and entertaining. My anxiety is that she can still underperform in an interview or a professional conversation, especially if she feels (rightly or wrongly) under pressure. I only mention this because any such reticences do not represent Melissa as she really is.
>
> Please let me know if I can be of further assistance.

1. The writer is obviously concerned about the impression the candidate might make and wants to reassure the reader that the candidate is really a good catch. Do you think the writer dealt with concerns fairly? Do you think the writer has helped the candidate?

2. Do you think the end of the letter was the best place to discuss the writer's concerns?

Sometimes we think so highly of a candidate that we write a letter of recommendation that makes the candidate seem too good to be true. If a very strong, positive letter is justified, then it is important to reassure the reader that the candidate is as good as you have described him or her to be.

Task Twenty-Two

What do you think of these forms of reassurance to a reader that the candidate is truly outstanding? Which might you accept, and which not?

1. I know this letter describes a person who seems too good to be true, but I can assure you that Shaw is very, very, very exceptional.

2. I realize that this letter is extremely positive and enthusiastic, but in my many years of teaching, I have seen only one other student as outstanding as Anand.

3. I have seen Vadim evolve over the years into a creative, self-motivated researcher who has taken on a leadership role in our research group. I can easily foresee how this young scholar will someday make a major contribution to his chosen area of study.

4. There have been rather few students for whom I could write such a positive letter of recommendation. I am pleased to be able to support Marie in her pursuit of a graduate career.

Language Focus: Double Meanings in Recommendations

As a lighthearted exercise, study these ambiguous recommendation statements that, from time to time, have been circulated on the Internet and in other places. Can you figure out the two meanings, one positive and one negative, that can be attached to each of these?

1. You will be lucky if you can get this person to work for you.
2. I am pleased to say this candidate is a former colleague of mine.
3. I would urge you to waste no time in making this candidate an offer.
4. This candidate is an unbelievable worker.
5. I most enthusiastically recommend this candidate with no qualifications whatsoever.
6. I can assure you that no person would be better for the job.

A further example of an ambiguous recommendation is given. It is our modernized version of a famous letter of recommendation written originally in French by the famous French statesman Cardinal Richelieu (1585–1642) to the French ambassador in Rome about a messenger on his way to Rome.

To Whom It May Concern

1. I am writing this letter for Mr. Charles Green,

2. a colleague at this institution,

3. who has asked for one. Mr. Green is the most

4. intelligent, talented and least

5. difficult of all my past and present colleagues.

6. He impresses everybody he meets.

7. I have often written supportive letters for him,

8. because of my high regard for him, not

9. because he has put me under pressure to do so.

10. We would be very sorry to lose him.

11. I think it is my responsibility to suggest to you

12. in your own best long-term interests

13. to pay very serious attention to Charles Green,

14. for then will emerge talent rather than

15. a person unworthy of a senior position with you.

16. I could offer more praise, but

17. I believe I have communicated my true opinion.

Honestly yours,

Eileen Over

Now that you have read the letter, read it again, reading only the odd numbered lines to reveal the true recommendation! Cardinal Richelieu used the same device; reading down his open two-pane letter said one thing, while reading across the two pages communicated something quite different. Participants in our classes often say that such ambiguities are possible in their languages. Chinese students point out, for example, that the true opinion can be obtained by reading only the first characters in Mandarin sentences.

And as a final point, instructors sometimes ask their students to write their own letters of recommendation, which the instructors then edit, print out on department notepaper, and sign. Although we don't approve of this practice, we know it occurs, more commonly in some cultures than in others. As instructors, we think it better to decline to write letters for students you do not really know, or at least we need to make sure you are provided with sufficient information to make a reasonable job of the task.

Task Twenty-Three

By now we think you are in a strong position to write a useful recommendation letter. One option is to draft your letter for one of the individuals whose CV you can find in the final section; another option is to write a letter for a fellow student or colleague.

Supporting the Publication Process

DREAMS OF ACADEMIC GLORY

```
"Dear Mr. Singh:

We would be delighted to publish your paper.  Not only
that, but we have decided that your beautifully
written submission letter is publishable as well. "
```

This penultimate section deals with communications that form part of the publication process. The final subsection also covers the "end game" of constructing acknowledgments for theses and dissertations.

Manuscript Submissions

Let us hope that your previous academic communications have helped you assemble a paper for possible publication. You have selected a journal and now need to post a short submission message (or cover letter) to the editorial email address of that journal. We are thus presuming that your manuscript will today be submitted electronically; in all cases, however, the accompanying message should be professional and usually brief. In particular, it should focus on the basic information the editor will be looking for.

Task Twenty-Four

Two versions of a simple submission message follow. Compare them, discuss them with a partner (if possible), and then try to anticipate the editor's reactions.

Letter A

Dear Dr. Carduner,

First of all, let me introduce myself to you. My name is _____, Assistant Professor of Finance, working at _____ University, a leading institution in my country. I have written several articles on microfinancing, and I would now like to contribute the enclosed paper to your distinguished journal. I hope you will be able to include it in a forthcoming issue. Please make any corrections you think necessary.

I look forward to hearing from you as soon as possible

Sincerely

Letter B

Dear Dr. Carduner,

I would like to submit to your journal for possible publication the enclosed paper entitled "Microfinancing in Rural Bangladesh: Causes of Microenterprise Success and Failure." The specific subject of this paper has not been submitted for publication elsewhere; it is partly based upon research performed for the completion of my PhD thesis.

I look forward to hearing from you in due course.

Sincerely

How would the editor react?

1. *Letter A engages in a considerable amount of* credentialism *("leading institution in my country"; "written several articles"). It is more about the author than about the paper.*

2. *Letter A does not give the actual title of the paper, while Letter B does.*

3. *The author of A suggests that the editor make any necessary corrections.*

4. *Letter B's closing phrase is* in due course, *while Letter A's is* as soon as possible. *(B's closing phrase is British; Americans will probably prefer* at your convenience.*)*

5. *Letter A does not clearly state that it has not been submitted elsewhere, but Letter B does.*

6. *Letter B mentions it is partly based on PhD research.*

There are a number of other administrative matters that may arise, occasionally at the time of submission, but more often subsequently. These are really beyond the scope of this small book, but we mention them briefly here.

A. Recommending reviewers

Many journals allow this. Here is the American Sociological Review: *"In your cover letter, you may recommend specific reviewers (or identify individuals that ASR should not use). Do not recommend colleagues, collaborators, or friends." So, one strategy might be to look at the list of people you have cited, and choose one leading figure, one well-published researcher, and one junior scholar. Alternatively or additionally, take advice from an appropriate senior member of your department. Or finally, decide not to recommend anybody.*

B. Charges and fees

Journals in many fields outside the humanities and social sciences now require authors to pay page charges when an article in accepted, and some journals are now requiring authors to pay a submission fee (often of

$75 or $100) on acceptance. Often the first few pages (say, 6–10) will be free, but after that substantial fees may be imposed; for example, the Journal of the Optical Society of America *charged in 2010, $220 for each extra printed page. In a second instance, the* Astronomical Journal *charged (again in 2010) $110 for every printed page. Both journals have considerable extra charges for printing color figures. As you can see, substantial costs can be involved. However, if you have no access to research grants or you are in some other disadvantaged position, such as working in a lesser developed country, you can always write to the editor explaining why it is difficult for you to pay the charges and fees. This may work.*

C. Treatment of animal or human subjects

If your work has involved human or animal subjects, you may need to assure the editor that you have followed the established guidelines for your area.

D. Use of proprietary (or commercial) material

If such substances have been used, you may need to clarify that you have permission for their use.

E. Possible conflicts of interest

Recent scandals in the newspapers about the financing of medical research by large pharmaceutical companies have led several journals to be more cautious about this. You may need to disclose sources of financing.

F. Multiple authors

If there are a large number of co-authors, editors may require assurance that each co-author played some significant part in the research. You should also indicate who will be the corresponding author.

Task Twenty-Five

Draft an appropriate submission letter to accompany one of your manuscripts.

Responding to Reviewers and Editors

Okay, you have submitted your manuscript. Now you wait for the review process to unfold. The process usually looks like this (Feak, 2009):

Stage 1: A quick review by the editor, possibly leading to what is called a "desk rejection" by the editor herself. For example, the article may be much too long, have obvious methodological weaknesses, or not meet established guidelines for submission.

Stage 2: Hopefully, though, it will be forwarded to two or three reviewers thought to be experts in the topic.

Stage 3: Reviewer responses received by the editor are forwarded to you, along with the editor's cover letter. This last will contain the decision: (a) Accept (this means usually with relatively minor revisions); (b) Revise and Resubmit (perhaps the most common outcome for many journals); and (c) Reject. It may also contain advice as to how best to proceed, perhaps along with some words of encouragement. However, remember that "an invitation to revise is not a guarantee of publication; rather it is an indication that the manuscript has the potential to be published, if it can be sufficiently improved to meet the expectations of the reviewers and editor" (Feak, 2009).

Stage 4: If the decision is (a) or (b) above, you revise appropriately and prepare a detailed response for the editor explaining what you have done, not done, and why.

Stage 5: The material is reviewed again by the editor, as well as often by the reviewer who had the most critical comments to make.

Stage 6: The editor sends a letter to you, offering Acceptance (with perhaps small further revisions), Further Revision, or Rejection (usually rare at this stage).

So let's consider what we might do when in *Stage 3* we get a "revise and re-submit" response.

Doubtless, you had worked hard on your submission; indeed, in some sense, it may have dominated your mental life for several months. You now get the responses from the journal, which recommends "Revise and resubmit"; further, at least one of the reviewers is fairly critical. Do not overreact to the criticism. Think about the long-term prospects and big picture. Follow this well-known proverbial advice: In Italian (in translation) "The night brings (good) advice"; In Russian, "Morning is wiser than evening"; and in Farsi, "Morning comes and goodness comes." So, put the responses aside for a day or two until you have calmed down.

As you plan your revisions, remember that the great majority of reviewers have used their considerable expertise to help you improve your manuscript. In most cases, they are trying to be fair and insightful and, in doing so, are bringing considerable scholarship to the task, even if their writing style may be relatively informal. In effect, they have entered into a dialogue with your manuscript. Finally, remember that the reviewers will concentrate on what they think needs changing, not on sections that they find acceptable, or even admirable. As a result, the reviews may look more negative than they really are.

As you plan your revisions, it is quite probable that the reviewers (and editor) will offer conflicting advice. Here are some examples.

- Reviewer 1 (R1) wants a stronger literature review; Reviewer 2 (R2) wants a more focused approach: "This is not a review article, so we don't need 70 references."
- R2 asks for more detail with regard to methodology; R1 and R3 do not.
- R3 thinks that the scientific claims in the Discussion are not fully supported by the evidence, while R1 wants you to finish up with some stronger practical recommendations.
- R2 wants more discussion about how the findings relate to theory; on the other hand, the editor concludes that "this is a straightforward 'normal science' empirical study that offers some new evidence; focus on this."

Obviously, some diplomacy is involved in this not atypical scenario. One strategy is to follow the recommendations that are the easiest for you to carry out, and then deal with the rest as best you can. And don't forget you can always argue that you cannot make all the suggested changes within the word (or character) limit that the journal requires. Here is an example from a manuscript on thoracic surgery:

Reviewer's comment:

I would suggest some further discussion on the benefits of VATS.

Author's response:

The advantages of VATS have been very well documented elsewhere. Such a discussion would add to the length of the paper, which Reviewer 2 has suggested reducing. We have added one reference that explores the advantages, but have not changed the text otherwise.

Stage 4

You have now revised, and it is time to resubmit your manuscript and send an accompanying message to the editor.

Task Twenty-Six

Which of these do you think are appropriate for a letter written to accompany a reviewed and revised manuscript? Discuss with a partner if possible.

1. I have revised the manuscript according to the reviewers' comments. Thanks for your attention.

2. I have revised the manuscript, and below please find a summary of the main changes made.

3. Please find below a detailed list of the changes to the manuscript that have been made. I hope the revision meets with your approval.

4. I would like to thank the reviewers for their helpful comments. In the commentary that follows, I have addressed each of the suggested changes and indicated how I have done this.

5. I am really grateful to your excellent reviewers for their insightful comments on my humble manuscript. I have worked extremely hard over the last two weeks in order to incorporate their wonderful suggestions. As you can see from the remainder of this response and from a re-reading of my heavily revised manuscript, I have done my very best to follow almost all of them. Thank you once again for giving me the opportunity to improve my submission to your famous journal.

Now let's look at an actual example. It is taken from a U.S. medical journal and concerns an article submitted from Japan dealing with a surgical procedure called mediastinoscopy (a small cut is made in the neck and a thin scope is inserted to examine the lungs for problems.)

Reviewer's Comment

> p. 11. The authors state that "it is neither practical nor economically justifiable to recommend mediastinoscopy for all candidates for surgery." This may be the authors' belief, but many surgeons do find it practical and justifiable to perform mediastinoscopy for all lung cancer patients.

Task Twenty-Seven

Which of the proposed responses by the authors do you prefer, and why?

> A. p. 11. We have rewritten as follows: "Since it is neither practical nor economical to recommend mediastinoscopy for all candidates for surgery, we developed indication criteria for cervical mediastinoscopy."

> B. p. 11. Reviewer 2 objected to our statement about the justifiability of routine mediastinoscopy.

> Response: This procedure remains a point of controversy within thoracic surgery. On p. 11 we have qualified our stance by saying: "It is neither practical nor economical in Japan to recommend mediastinoscopy for all candidates for surgery." Regardless of opinions on this issue, we believe everyone would agree that it is better to avoid this procedure if the same information can be obtained non-invasively at much lower cost.

> C. p. 11. An all-too-typical response from the American surgical establishment focused, as it is, both on maximizing profits and reducing the chances of expensive malpractice lawsuits. In international terms, we stick to our original position.

A second actual example is taken from a reviewer's more general comments about a manuscript submitted to a journal dealing with writing research. The manuscript was written by two corpus linguists who attempted to show how a particular free software package could be easily adopted for writing research and who then illustrated how the resulting techniques could produce an interesting large-scale analysis of sentence-initial *This* in a corpus of student writing. While R1 was broadly happy to recommend acceptance, R2 opted for "revise and resubmit" at best. Here is the first of R2's major criticisms:

> A weakness lies in the absence of theory about writing, writing development, teaching or writing instruction. In what way could (cognitive, social, developmental) writing research benefit from the insight acquired by corpus analysis?

Task Twenty-Eight

A discussion between the two corpus linguist authors led them to consider these possible responses to the criticism from R2. Which do you prefer? And what do you think actually happened?

Option A

> We will withdraw the paper and resubmit it to a journal more open to corpus linguistic research.

Option B

> We will agree and, for the first time in our lives, study the writing research literature in order to try to answer the criticisms.

Option C

> We will accept all of R1's suggestions, as well as some of R2's points. But on the major one quoted above, we will argue back and say to the editor:
>
> > We think R2 is essentially missing the point. Our main aim was not to make any contribution to writing research theory, but to offer an introduction to useful methodological tools that may be new to many members of the writing research community and to present a case study showing how the tools and techniques can be implemented. We believe that the decision is yours.

Option D

> We will recruit a third author who is a writing research expert.

Language Focus: Politely Standing Your Ground

In the previous papers we have seen authors explaining why they do not always agree with reviewers' comments. Choosing the phraseology for arguing back can be important. You want to make your point, but you need to do so with civility and sensitivity. Here are a few language options that you might find helpful:

Reviewer B's criticism on p. 3, para 3.

1. *While we can see why Reviewer B objected to your statement here, on balance we prefer to keep our original formulation for the following reasons: . . .*

2. *With regard to this particular criticism, after considerable reflection, we believe what we wrote is tenable, especially following the additional supporting evidence provided by the recent paper by. . . . , which we have added to the references.*

3. *On this point there is clearly room for a difference of opinion, and we have carefully considered B's alternative interpretation of the situation. We have added "probably" to indicate that some doubt remains, but believe that the evidence continues to support our original position.*

4. *Reviewer B's criticism is interesting, but would seem to involve a slight misinterpretation of our position, and here we might note that neither of the other reviewers had any difficulty with accepting our claim. We have added a further reference (which supports our position) to indicate that our interpretation of the data is in no way idiosyncratic.*

Now here are some general guidelines for correspondence with the editor:

1. Remember that an invitation to revise is usually a positive sign. So do not take criticisms personally.

2. Read the editor's letter and the reviewers' comments carefully.

3. If the editor suggests getting help with the English, choose someone who has some understanding of your research area as well as a good knowledge of the language.

4. Respond to each of the major comments. (Minor ones such as spelling corrections or corrections to references do not need detailed commentary.)

5. In your response, help the editor by using detailed references to the text, such as "p. 2 first para."

6. Thank people for useful suggestions, but do not automatically defer to the editor or reviewers. If you disagree with a comment, explain why.

7. If you have made additional changes not suggested by the reviewers, briefly explain what they are and why you have made them.

8. If you have been asked to revise and resubmit, do so as quickly as is convenient.

9. Explain what you are doing about any page charges or fees, if this is appropriate.

10. If you do not plan to revise, inform the editor of your decision.

Task Twenty-Nine

Here is a response letter. In your view, how well does it follow the guidelines given?

> Dear Dr. _____
>
> Thank you for your recent letter regarding our manuscript entitled _____ . We are pleased that you have asked us to revise and resubmit our work to *The Annals of Thoracic Surgery*. In accordance with your recommendations and those of the reviewers we have made the following changes to the manuscript.
>
> 1. Reviewer 1 suggested that the title be shortened. We have done this.
> 2. Reviewer 1 asked if. . . . Unfortunately, . . .
> 3. Reviewer 3 thought that the number of illustrations could be reduced. We agree and have deleted Figures 5 and 7. The remaining figures have been renumbered . . .
>
> [A further seven points that the authors addressed, but omitted here.]
>
> We thank the reviewers for their thoughtful and careful review of our manuscript and hope that these changes will make the manuscript suitable for publication. If any additional changes are necessary, please let us know and we will respond immediately. If the paper is now acceptable to you, we can confirm that we are in a position to pay any page charges.
>
> Sincerely,

Finally on a Lighter Note

We know that receiving a rejection letter or even one that requires an arduous "revise and resubmit" process can cause a strong emotional response. We, therefore, close this section with several paragraphs from a letter to the editor published in the *American Journal of Radiology* on April Fool's Day, 1992. The fact that it has been republished in several other journals since shows how well it resonates with the authors of manuscripts. It has also proved to be a great success in our workshops.

Dear Sir, Madame or Other,

Enclosed is our latest version of MS#85-02-22-RRRRR, that is, the re-re-revised revision of our paper. Choke on it. We have again rewritten the entire manuscript from start to finish. We even changed the goddarn running head! Hopefully, we have suffered enough by now to satisfy even you and your bloodthirsty reviewers.

I shall skip the usual point by point description of every single change we made in response to the critiques. After all, it is fairly clear that your reviewers are less interested in details of scientific procedures than in working out their personality problems and sexual frustrations by seeking some kind of demented glee in the sadistic and arbitrary exercise of tyrannical power over hapless authors like ourselves who happen to fall into their clutches. We do understand that, in view of the misanthropic psychopaths you have on your editorial board, you need to keep sending them papers, for if they aren't receiving manuscripts they'd probably be out mugging old ladies or clubbing baby seals to death. Still, from this batch of reviewers, C was clearly the most hostile and we request that you do not ask him, or her, to review this revision. Indeed, we have mailed letter bombs to four or five people we suspect of being reviewer C, so if you send the manuscript back to them the review process could be unduly delayed.

. . .

We hope that you will be pleased with this revision and will finally recognize how urgently deserving of publication this work is. If not, then you are an unscrupulous, depraved monster with no shred of human decency. You ought to be in a cage. May whatever heritage you come from be the butt of the next round of ethnic jokes. If you accept it, however, we wish to thank you for your patience and wisdom throughout this process and to express our appreciation of your scholarly insights. To repay we would be happy to review some manuscripts for you; please send us the next manuscript that any of these reviewers submit to your journal.

Assuming you accept this paper, we would also like to add a footnote acknowledging your help with this manuscript and to point out that we liked the paper much better the way we originally wrote it, but you held the editorial shotgun to our heads and forced us to chop, restate, hedge, expand, shorten, and in general convert a meaty paper into stir-fry vegetables. We couldn't, or wouldn't, have done it without your input.

Roy F. Baumeister

Case Western Reserve University, Cleveland, Ohio, 44106

Journal Biostatements

After your paper has been accepted, you may be asked to provide a brief biostatement to be printed as part of your article. Although they are also autobiographical, biostatements constitute a very different genre to those of Statements of Purpose or Personal Statements. They are short, to the point, and impersonal. They vary in length from a single sentence to a short paragraph of usually fewer than a hundred words. Biostatements of article authors may occur in journal articles (our multidisciplinary survey suggests that about 25 percent of journals print biostatements), or as part of speaker information on conference programs, in departmental newsletters, or, increasingly, on departmental websites.

Here is an example (written in fewer than 80 words):

Christine B. Feak is a Lecturer IV in the English Language Institute at the University of Michigan in Ann Arbor. She is the co-author of several articles and textbooks, the latest being *Academic Interactions* (with S. Reinhart and T. Rohlck) and *Telling a Research Story* (with J. M. Swales), both published by the University of Michigan Press. She is a member of the editorial boards of *The English for Specific Purposes Journal* and *Journal of English for Academic Purposes.*

We can notice here that there are no first-person pronouns, and no evaluative language, such as, *She is well-known internationally for her writing workshops.* Everything then depends on the choice of the factual material to include. (But note that this may not be always true of departmental websites, which sometimes offer more personal perspectives.)

According to Tardy and Swales (2011), these biostatements tend to follow a set pattern. Elements in parenthesis may or may not occur.

Describe Position

(Confirm PhD and state where from)

Summarize publications

List major research areas

Mention key professional activities

(Describe honors, etc.)

Task Thirty

Either construct a biostatement for yourself, or edit this entry and reduce it from its current 85 words to a maximum of 60 words.

John M. Swales was the director of the English Language Institute from 1985 to 2001. Previously, he worked at universities in England and Africa. He officially retired as a professor of Linguistics in 2006. His most recent publications are *Telling a Research Story: Writing a Literature Review* (with C. Feak) and *Incidents in an Educational Life: A Memoir (of Sorts),* both published by Michigan Press in 2009. He remains a faculty advisor to the MICASE project. In 2004, he received an honors PhD from Uppsala.

Writing Acknowledgments

There has been considerable research into acknowledgments in the last two decades, some by information scientists (e.g., Cronin, 1995) and some by applied linguists (e.g., Giannoni, 2002; Hyland, 2004; and Gesuato, 2004). Part of this work has focused on acknowledgments in research articles and part on acknowledgments in theses and dissertations. A major motive for all these investigations lies in the fact that acknowledgments offer public recognition of some of the networks and relationships that underlie the research process. Interview research by Cronin and others also suggests that acknowledgments are widely read. Indeed, some years ago we asked a senior applied linguist which part of a research paper he read first, and he replied, "the acknowledgments." When we expressed surprise at this, he replied, "Well, I want to know who has been talking to whom."

Journal Acknowledgments

We deal with these first. Here are some findings from the available literature:

- Acknowledgments are becoming increasingly common and are becoming longer in length.
- Acknowledgments in the "hard" sciences tend to focus on financial and technical support, including access to data or materials.
- Acknowledgments in the "soft" sciences and the humanities tend to focus on intellectual and academic assistance (such as thanking reviewers for their suggestions).
- A recent study of medical journals shows an average length of acknowledgments of around 85 words.
- If allowed, there is a strong preference for using *I* for single authors and *we* for multiple authors rather than third person forms such as *the present authors.*
- After acknowledging multiple sources of help, only a minority of texts conclude with a disclaimer such as, *However, any remaining errors are my own.*

- Acknowledgments usually occur at the foot of the first page. Sometimes, however, they can occur just before the references, as in, for example, some aerospace and anthropology journals.

Task Thirty-One

Read this acknowledgments text, and answer the questions.

①The authors wish to thank Tom H._____, Carole W._____, and Elizabeth Z._____ for their helpful comments at various stages of this project. ②We thank Raymond D._____, The Center for Public Opinion at _____, and the Election Study Center at _____ for use of their survey data. ③However, they bear no responsibility for our interpretation of the data. ④We are also indebted to the University of _____ and the John T _____ Center for _____ for their financial assistance with this project.

1. What field do you think this text is taken from?

2. The people mentioned here are expressed differently from the authors cited in the body of the research article (RA). What is the difference—and why?

3. How have the authors ordered their acknowledgments?

4. How is the *disclaimer* expressed?

5. Suppose the authors also wanted to acknowledge the reviewers. How might they express this statement, and where might they put it?

6. Suppose you want to add that an earlier version of this project was presented at a conference. What you would write, and where would you place it?

Language Focus: Expressions of Gratitude

As a bridge between the shorter acknowledgments in RAs and the longer ones in theses and dissertations, consider these different ways of expressing gratitude. It is important to offer some variety in the thanking expressions you use. We have divided them into **basic** and **follow-up** expressions of gratitude.

Basic

I am very thankful to X for Y.

I am deeply grateful to X for Y.

I would like to offer my sincere thanks to X for Y.

I would like to express my deep gratitude to X for Y.

I am indebted to X for Y.

I owe a great deal to X for Y.

I owe a debt of gratitude to X for Y.

I am pleased to acknowledge the support of X for Y.

Follow-Up

Special gratitude is also extended to X for Y.

Many thanks are also due to X for Y.

My heartfelt appreciation also goes out to X for Y.

Another way of varying expressions of gratitude is to change the word order (Gesuato, 2004), as in:

I would like to thank Jane Fountain for her generous help.

For her generous help, I would like to thank Jane Fountain.

Some writers try to avoid the repetition of these phrases by opting for a **list format.** Here is a good example:

> I would like to offer my sincerest thanks to my committee members: to the Chair, A___ B___, for his wise counsel and direction; to C___ D___, who has for many years supported and encouraged me; to E___ F___ for always answering my inquiries so promptly; and to G___ H___ for his time and help in working out certain technical problems.

We dare say that the acknowledgments writer's nightmare is to inadvertently leave somebody out who ought to have been included. Some writers try to avoid possible offense by offering a generalized statement of thanks at the outset. Here is a nice example:

> It would be difficult to acknowledge everyone who has in some way or another contributed to the research reported in this dissertation.

Theses and Dissertation Acknowledgments

At least in the United States, theses and dissertation acknowledgments, for obvious reasons, are not an examinable part of a master's thesis or doctoral dissertation. What is written is entirely at the discretion of the writer.

However, the unexamined nature of the acknowledgments can present some dangers, perhaps especially for the non-native speaker of English. On a macro level, there is a need to strike a balance between not saying enough (possibly suggesting ingratitude) and giving too much praise and thanks to everybody else (possibly suggesting that there is little of yourself in the dissertation). On the micro level, since the acknowledgments come at the beginning of a thesis or dissertation, mistakes and infelicities in them can create a negative first impression. Clearly then, it is important for you to have your acknowledgments reviewed and discussed by a friend or colleague before it is too late. Taking this step is also a way of making sure that you don't leave anybody out who should have been acknowledged! On the other hand, it is worth remembering that this is the one place where your own voice can be heard, uninfluenced by your academic mentors.

In our experience, master's theses acknowledgments in the United States tend to be quite short, while those prefacing dissertations can be quite long, especially those written by Americans in the "softer" fields. Hyland (2004) studied acknowledgments in Hong Kong master's and doctoral theses; the average word length for the former was 117 and for the latter 205. In both cases, there are usually several people and several organizations to be thanked, and it is important to find a range of ways of expressing gratitude.

Task Thirty-Two

Here is a draft of the acknowledgments in a master's thesis. Some words have been left out; which of the choices given after the text would you recommend?

ACKNOWLEDGMENTS

First and foremost, I would like to ① _____ my profound gratitude to the Royal Thai Government, specifically to the Ministry of Foreign Affairs, for granting me support to ② _____ my graduate studies. The support has given me not only a future career, but also opportunities to ③ _____ to higher education abroad, to work on a project I am interested in, and to prepare myself to better serve my country and society.

There are two people whom I would like to ④ _____ individually. First, I am deeply grateful to Professor L., my thesis advisor, for her encouragement, and careful and wise guidance of my project. Secondly, I ⑤ _____ a great deal to Professor Y., my second reader, whose supervision and advice ⑥ _____ substantially to my study.

Finally, I ⑦ _____ to thank all my friends in Ann Arbor who have always supported me in every way, especially in the ⑧ _____ of this project.

(Luejit, minor editing)

1. communicate/express/offer

2. pursue/obtain/follow

3. be open/be confronted/be exposed

4. introduce/cite/acknowledge

5. have/owe/offer

6. has devoted/ has helped/has contributed

7. want/need/would like

8. carrying through/completion/undertaking

As the Language Focus on Expressions of Gratitude (see pages 79–80) and the Task Thirty-One make very clear, there are strong phraseological conventions and expectations in these types of text. In addition, there are matters of judgment here about the level of indebtedness the writer wishes to express.

Task Thirty-Three

We think that the three extracts from these acknowledgments are each, in different ways, not quite right. Can you identify the weaknesses in each?

A. The author wishes to express his deep and sincere appreciation to the Co-Chairpersons of his doctoral committee, Professor K. and Professor M., not only for their valuable advice and unfailing guidance, but also for providing oral support and encouragement during a frustrating period. The author is deeply and forever grateful to both of them.

B. I am enormously grateful to the Institute and to its then director, A. Even more significant was the field research fellowship awarded to me by the R. I cannot put into words my appreciation for the many facilities put at my disposal by the Director—Dr. P. The office's staff members received me with open arms and . . . .

C. Writing this dissertation has given me opportunities not only for strengthening my academic achievement but also for understanding American people and culture. Thus it has been exciting and challenging for me to carry out research on small-town America's neighborhood quality of life. . . .

We have already seen in Task Thirty-two that Luejit, as a Thai civil servant, began by showing her allegiance to her government; students from certain other cultures have pointed out that their traditions would require them to mention support from their immediate families first. In general, however, U.S. dissertation acknowledgments tend to follow this structure:

1. Dissertation committee (advisors/supervisors)
2. Other university people playing a role
3. Financial support
4. Fellow students
5. Other special friends
6. Family

Task Thirty-Four

If relevant, write a draft of your acknowledgments for your thesis, dissertation, or research paper.

Moving On to an Academic or Research Career

The final section of this small book deals with some of the written genres that you are likely to become involved with as you move on from your graduate education or from a temporary post-doc position. (However, we recognize that you have probably needed a CV long before this—a fact we have indicated by earlier references to this section.) We deal in order with CVs, external job applications, and Statements of Teaching Philosophy. This order approximately reflects what many people feel to be an increasing level of uncertainty about these communications. However, these days a certain amount of Internet searching will usually turn up many pieces of useful advice.

Curricula Vitae

A *curriculum vitae* (CV), Latin for "course of life," is an account in note form of your education and career. (Note that in British English the abbreviation "c.v." is often used.) Your CV is a living document in that it continues to change and grow along with your experiences. Senior researchers may have CVs extending over many pages, while junior researchers will need fewer pages. As with many of the other genres discussed in this book, CVs will exhibit some cultural variation, which you may want to take into account as you prepare or update your vitae or revise it for a specific job application.

Task Thirty-Five

Consider these talking points about CVs; in so doing, assume a U.S. destination for your CV. Work through the points with a partner if possible. Indicate whether you agree, disagree, or are unsure or you and a partner do not agree.

+ = agree

— = disagree.

? = unsure (or my partner and I don't agree)

_____ 1. A resume and a CV are the same genre.

_____ 2. You should include your date of birth, sex, and nationality.

_____ 3. Your CV should include both your home and departmental address.

_____ 4. It is best to use reverse chronological order throughout (i.e., put the most recent things first).

_____ 5. The longer your CV, the better.

_____ 6. Provide some information about your high school.

_____ 7. List only advanced or special courses you have taken.

_____ 8. List computer skills or expertise in using special equipment.

_____ 9. Put your name in much larger font at the top.

_____ 10. Do not try to "translate" degrees that have no exact equivalent in the United States (Diplom in Germany, D.E.A in France, M.Phil. in Britain).

This task has been designed to raise your awareness about some of the options facing someone writing a CV suitable for an academic or research position. With this as background, now consider how you might respond to the material in Task Thirty-Six.

Task Thirty-Six

Here is a typical CV written by an American citizen in 2010 for a U.S. audience. What do you like and dislike about it? What suggestions might you make to Robin Lee?

Robin S. Lee

Department of Biology   e-mail: rsl@morch.xxx.edu

3039 Watson Hall   URL: www.xxx.morc.emap.~js/

Central State University   (555) 555-0000

Centerville, OH 12345-6789

Education

2009–present   Doctoral candidate in Molecular Biology

                      Central State University, Centerville, OH

                      (Degree expected summer 2013)

2007   MS in Biology, Southeastern State

                      University, Southville, MA

                      Thesis: Protein Folding of Alcohol

                      Dehydrogenase

2005   BS in Biology, Eastern State University,

                      Buffalo, NY (GPA 3.7)

Research Experience

Fall 2010–present   Research assistant: DNA isolation from

                           fungal specimens with Dr. R. Anderson

Fall 2009–summer 2010   Research assistant: Electron microscopy of

                           dried mycological specimens. PI, Dr. F.

                           Guzman.

Summer 2006   Field assistant: Southeastern State University Biological Station

Teaching Experience

Fall 2010   Laboratory instructor for Introductory Biology, Central State University

Full teaching responsibilities for one undergraduate section of 18 students

Winter 2006   Teaching assistant for Anatomy and Physiology: Southeastern State University

Full teaching responsibilities for one undergraduate section of 26 students

Fall 2005   Lab assistant for Physiology and Development: Southeastern State University

Assisted students with weekly lab projects and answered student questions

Publications   F. Guzman and R. S. Lee. *Morchella asci* Ultrastructure. *Mycologia* (in press).

Conference Presentations

Summer 2010   R. S. Lee and F. Guzman. Ultrastructure of *Morchella asci*. Poster presentation at AIBS, Baltimore, MD.

Honors and Awards

2008   *Journal of Cell Science* Travel Award

2006   Southeastern State University Research Foundation Fellowship

As demonstrated in this CV, information for a U.S. audience is usually presented in reverse chronological order. However, if your academic and/or employment history has noticeable gaps (which may exist for any number of reasons) you may have more success with a *functional* CV—one that groups your skills and achievements into sections, thus highlighting your skills rather than focusing on specific work titles and dates. For example, you may have subsections that focus on laboratory skills or equipment that you can use, which can be presented as a sequence of activities and achievements.

Language Focus: Gapping in CVs

Gapping is a technical term for the deletion of certain linguistic elements, such as in diary writing like, **went for walk and saw a fox**. In a CV, gapped phrases may be preferred over full sentences so that information is conveyed using the smallest number of words necessary.

The elements most likely to be gapped in CVs are first-person pronouns, auxiliary verbs, articles, relative clause elements (e.g., **courses taught** rather than **courses I have taught,** and certain prepositional phrases). Thus, gapped phrases such as these are common in CVs:

1. fluent in Mandarin
2. taught advanced-level calculus
3. coordinated and implemented two research projects
4. conducted data analysis
5. designed Web pages for Introduction to Psychology (2007–2009)
6. duties included maintaining lab equipment
7. accompanied students on 2010 geology field trip
8. helped construct interactive database
9. coded transcripts using Resourcer program
10. languages spoken: Spanish, English, Portuguese
11. courses taught: Latin American History, Mexico Today
12. grants received: 2010–2011, Rivera Grant ($12,000) for archival research

Notice that in the last three cases, the participle follows the subject. This is because the gapped elements include active auxiliary verbs and relative clause elements. The full forms would be

10a. Languages that I can speak / have spoken:

11a. Courses that I have taught: . . .

12a. Grants that I have received: . . .

Placing the participle in pre-position could result in some confusion. For instance, a reader might think that **taught courses** (compare to 11 above) are **courses that were taught to you.**

Finally and more important, note that gapping not only reduces the number of words but also makes your CV more impressive. The elimination of all those first-person references makes the CV appear less "egocentric," and the use of verbs makes your life story more achievement- and action-oriented. (Compare **Instructor for advanced-level calculus** with **Taught advanced-level calculus.**)

Task Thirty-Seven

Take this short text that focuses on teaching experience, and rewrite it so that it would be suitable for a CV. Be sure to make up a subheading, too.

My first year (2007) in the Chemistry Department as a beginning grad student I worked in the Chemistry Tutorial Center, a center that provided one-on-one help to students in any Chemistry class. As a tutor I helped students from Introduction to Chemistry (Chem 100) as well as those from senior level Organic Chemistry (Chem 415). I have been a teaching assistant for the Department of Chemistry since 2008. During that time I have taught a number of courses, including General and Inorganic Chemistry (Chem 125), Inorganic Chemistry (Chem 130), and Structure and Reactivity (Chem 210). I have been fully responsible for my own section of 210 each semester for the last year. I have really enjoyed my experiences as a teacher of chemistry and would like to continue teaching after I graduate.

There are often questions about what to include on a CV and how to include it. In this next task we introduce some interesting questions that have arisen in our classes.

Task Thirty-Eight

How would you handle the following (if at all). Work with a partner, if possible.

1. Your advisor asks you to give a talk based on your research to her graduate level class. She asks you to fill the full 50-minute period. If you decide to do so, how would you enter it on the CV?

2. Your advisor asks you to give a 20-minute talk on your experiences as a new graduate student. How might this be entered on the CV, if at all?

3. The final session of an advanced class or seminar is a poster session where all students showcase their work. Friends, colleagues, and all members of the department are also invited to attend. Is this a publication? A presentation? How would you include this?

4. Your university sponsors a biannual, informal poster session that provides an opportunity for doctoral students to present their dissertation ideas and research. Students must submit a poster proposal that is reviewed by a university-wide committee. Should this be considered a publication or a presentation? How would you include this?

5. The 200-word abstract of your conference presentation appears in the glossy conference program. Is this a publication? And if so, how will you cite it?

6. A 500-word report of the research you presented at a conference appears in the *New York Times*. How will you deal with this, if at all?

7. A student reporter from the university newspaper visits the lab where you work and discusses in some detail the work that you have been doing. Would you include this? If so, how?

8. You translate one of your published papers into your own language for a journal in your home country. In so doing, you make a few small changes to make it more accessible for the local readership. Is this a separate publication? What advice would you offer here?

External Job Applications

Most final year master's students are on the job market, looking for research positions in government, education, or industry. Those completing PhDs may be searching for post-doc, or academic positions as assistant professors (both tenure-track and visiting), or perhaps as instructors or lecturers.

In your field, which of the following would you expect to include in your application for an assistant professor position? (Y = Yes, N = No, ? = perhaps or sometimes)

_____ 1. A single-authored writing sample

_____ 2. Samples of co-authored publications

_____ 3. A short (half-page) cover letter

_____ 4. A long (two-page) job application letter

_____ 5. A statement of research interests

_____ 6. A statement of your teaching philosophy

_____ 7. A syllabus that you have designed

_____ 8. A sample lesson plan

_____ 9. A transcript (official copy)

_____ 10. Copies of Likert-scale teaching evaluations

Here is a model job application letter for a beginning position at a small liberal arts college. We have numbered the paragraphs for ease of reference. Following the letter, we have made a number of comments about these paragraphs.

Dr. Mary Gordon   456 Third Street

Chair, Search Committee   Central City

Department of Communication Sciences   CS 56122-3452

Raydown College

Raydown, IX 22222   November 1, 2010

Dear Dr. Gordon,

(1) I am writing to apply for the position of Assistant Professor of Psychology, as advertised in the *APA Monitor* (#73). I am currently a doctoral candidate in psychology at Central State University and plan to defend my dissertation in April or May next year. I am especially interested in this position because my primary teaching interests closely parallel those described in your advertisement.

(2) As you can see from my CV, I have had considerable teaching experience in a variety of areas. In fact, at this university I have taught courses in three departments: Psychology, Linguistics, and English. Last winter term, I was a teaching assistant for Developmental Psychology (Psych 268). My duties included designing the syllabus and assignments for my discussion sections, leading discussions, grading, and assisting student groups in their joint research projects. In the Department of Linguistics, I was first a TA for the introductory survey course (Linguistics 101), and then last summer I was given an opportunity to design and have full responsibility for a second-level introductory course in psycholinguistics, my principal area of specialization. More than half of the 27 students in this class were elementary school teachers in training and so I gave special attention to child language acquisition. Finally, I have

on three occasions taught writing-in-the-curriculum composition courses for the English Department, all three times focusing on writing in the social sciences. This last experience has helped me to rethink the role of writing in social science education and how this connects with ways of developing students' critical thinking and argumentation skills.

(3) I therefore believe that I could satisfy your department's teaching needs in a number of areas. Indeed, I would welcome an opportunity to teach introductory courses in developmental and cognitive psychology and other courses in language acquisition, psycholinguistics, and bilingualism. I also believe that my experiences in teaching social science writing and advising students on their projects will be valuable for your team-taught "Research Lab in Communication Sciences."

(4) My research interests are described more fully elsewhere, so I will only offer some highlights here. I am primarily interested in what children's conversations tell us about their thinking processes and about their beliefs about other people's thoughts (both children and adults). More specifically, I have focused on 8 to 10 year olds and how they justify, condemn, or explain the actions and behaviors of their peers. I use experimental techniques for this involving pairs of children watching videotaped episodes of other children's verbal explanations. In my dissertation, this data is then used to construct what we might call a 10 year old's "theory of mind." I argue that how far this "theory" is developed in this age group predicts their level of social adjustment and maturation. As the CV shows, I have already begun to present and publish my work in this area.

(5) My future research interests lie in expanding my dissertation in several directions. I am very interested in comparing the verbal justifications of my current research cohort with those of children of kindergarten age. Like many I am also acutely aware that the United States is becoming a more multicultural society, and I therefore want to examine

the verbal explanations of bilingual children and whether this group has a more or less evolved "theory of mind" than their monolingual counterparts. These research projects could very easily involve undergraduates who are interested in children's cognitive and linguistic development.

(6) I am enclosing a curriculum vitae and a summary of my dissertation for your consideration. I also enclose a separate sheet with the names of four people I have asked to supply letters of reference. If you need further information, I can be most easily reached at 734-555-7890 or by email (sandrap@xxx.edu). I thank you for your consideration and look forward to hearing from you.

Sincerely,

Sandra J. Pomona

Commentary

a. *In Para. 1 Sandra clearly explains her current status and why she is especially interested in this position. In this way, she shows she has read the advertisement carefully.*

b. *In Para. 2 she immediately jumps in with a full account of her teaching experiences to date. She stresses the variety of this experience and how she took on various responsibilities in this regard.*

c. *In the next paragraph, she follows up by indicating what she might teach at Raymond College. She is both clear here and yet suitably modest, as in* I therefore believe that I could satisfy . . . *and* I also believe that my experiences in teaching . . . will be valuable for. . . .

d. *In Para. 4, she moves on to summarizing her research achievements to date and follows this in the next paragraph, with an indication of her future research plans. This latter paragraph serves to indicate that she already possesses a coherent future research agenda and, more, one that is sensitive to the changing nature of American society.*

e. *In the closing paragraph, she provides the necessary details for future contacts, ending with a suitably open-ended,* I thank you for your consideration.

Task Thirty-Nine

If relevant, write an application letter for a position that you are or might be interested in. If this is not relevant, give Sandra some advice about her use of the letter for other job applications.

Sandra is also applying for two other positions. Position B is an assistant professor of psychology position at a major research university that is well known for its large and influential psychology department. Position C is a post-doc position in an institute for child development. Sandra contacts her advisor by email about Position B and asks, "Can I just send my original letter?" She receives this reply:

> Hi, Sandra. Please please rethink your letter, which BTW was just perfect for Raydown College. I know something of the dept in the Position B advert; these guys are serious researchers. So, at the least, reverse the order of the teaching and research paragraphs, and shorten a bit the former and lengthen the latter. You might also mention the kinds of research grants you might apply for, and what you might teach at the graduate level. And are there any famous profs there you might want to mention, and who might act as your "mentor"? So, I know it's a pain, but rethink.
>
> Best.

Now Sandra contacts you by email about the post-doc and asks, "Do I just drop the teaching stuff? And if so what should I add? What other changes?"

Write your advice to Sandra in the form of an email message.

Statements of Teaching Philosophy

Increasingly educational institutions are requesting Statements of Teaching Philosophy as part of job application packages (Coppola, 2002). Usually these can be quite short (often only one page), but that doesn't make them any easier to write! Perhaps the most important thing to remember about these statements is that somebody has asked for them. As a result, you are not only being asked to reflect on your past teaching and learning experiences in some elevated and general kind of way; you are also being asked to project yourself, at least indirectly, as a potential future employee of the institution to which you have applied. The hiring committee wants to get a sense of how you might "fit in." As a result, visit your target institution's website, particularly documents such as the *mission statement*. What is the balance between critical thinking and technical skills? What does it say about internationalism or interdisciplinarity? Is there a religious affiliation of any kind? Of course, do not try and directly imitate what is said on the website, but let it inform the way you tackle this tricky writing task. (And, of course, this means you might have to adjust your statement a bit for different kinds of school.)

Your statement will likely include several of the following;

1. your thoughts about how students learn
2. your thoughts about how instruction can best help student learning
3. your learning goals for students
4. your thoughts about how your teaching might further improve
5. your thoughts about how students (and instructors) might best be evaluated
6. Your beliefs about changing educational needs in today's world.

In a survey of search committee chairs, Meizlish & Kaplan (2008) found broad agreement that the chairs wanted to see:

- Evidence that candidates had thought about how to *enact* their teaching philosophies
- Evidence that candidates had *reflected* on teaching experiences
- Evidence that candidates were suitably *student-* or *learning-centered*
- Evidence that candidates could write in a *readable* manner (without too much jargon).

Task Forty

Read these short paragraph-length extracts from Statements of Teaching Philosophy, and then consider these two questions.

1. In which of the six categories would you place each extract?

2. If you were chair of the search committee in your current institution, would you rate each extract as: (a) very impressive (just what you are looking for); (b) adequate, but not very attention-getting; or (c) really very ordinary?

A.

The ultimate goal of engineering education is the teaching of applications that will aid in solving real-world problems. I am confident that if students believe what they learn in classes will be applicable to their future careers, they will appreciate the importance of lessons and thus engage themselves in the learning process more completely. Thus, the primary task of a teacher is to address the importance and applications of lessons to the students in his or her classes.

B.

The instructor and student should engage in an active dialog. However, it is easy to get carried away in a dialog with only a few students and forget you are facing a whole classroom. I have learned to always reflect aloud on the interactions with individual students for the whole class, so everybody can benefit from the discussion. I therefore try to encourage questions, and to respond to questions constructively. I believe a good question presents itself as a good teachable moment. Thus, I try to capture these "teachable moments" and relate them to the conceptual principles I want to convey.

C.

I see an inseparable link between research and teaching. Research informs teaching, and teaching, at least at the graduate level, informs research. So this link is beneficial for both parties. As the president of one major university once put it, "Instructors who don't do research are like extinct volcanoes." But with the link, students will learn new theories and their applications, which will be valuable for their future careers, while instructors will be motivated to conduct research.

D.

Of course I encountered the difficulty of facilitating discussion in a classroom of thirty bolted-down seats, many of which held students either unprepared or too shy to speak. Here, then, I must add a corollary to my first principle: facilitate different kinds of learning activity in the classroom. After attending two presentations by Professor Sam Freedman, I have decided to introduce elements of cooperative learning into the undergraduate classes I will be teaching in the future.

E.

Teaching is a creative act, an organizational activity, and a social contract. As a creative act, I see teaching as the root of all performance and communication, namely, to take ideas and feelings derived from my understanding of the world and create a situation in which others can understand what I see. As an organizational activity, I design learning environments in which others might develop the skills necessary to effectively construct and communicate their understandings of the world. As a social contract, I have a set of moral obligations that drive my actions and behaviors as one human being who exists within the communities of higher education.

Postscript

We have now reached the end of this short book and the end of the academic journey we have tried to assist you with. Of course, space limits have prevented us from covering every aspect of academic correspondence, and we could ideally have provided more detail about some of the genres that have been discussed. In particular, we have largely limited discussion to U.S. documents; this is partly because most of our experience has been in this part of the world, and partly because *Navigating Academia* is being published by a U.S. university press. Even so, we hope that instructors and users elsewhere will be able to adapt these materials to their own circumstances. And we wish everybody the best of luck as they make their way through their own academic worlds.

JMS & CBF

January 2011

References

Aull, L., & Barcy, K. (2010). *The "good," the "bad," and the snarky: Native and non-native student use of scare quotes in upper-level academic writing.* Conference on Intellectual Rhetoric, Georgia State University, Atlanta.

Axelson, E. (2003) *A longitudinal study of intercultural discourse in a master's thesis project group.* PhD Dissertation, the University of Michigan.

Barton, E., Ariail, J., & Smith. T. (2004). The professional in the personal: The genre of personal statements in residency applications. *Issues in Writing, 15,* 76–124.

Bekins, L. K., Huckin, T. N., & Kijak, L. (2004). The personal statement in medical school applications: Rhetorical structure in a diverse and unstable context. *Issues in Writing, 15,* 56–75.

Brown, R. M. (2004). Self-composed: Rhetoric in psychology personal statements. *Written Communication, 21,* 242–260.

Coppola, B. P. (2002) Writing a statement of teaching philosophy. *Journal of College Science Teaching, 31,* 448–453.

Cronin, B. (1995). *The scholar's courtesy: The role of acknowledgments in the primary communication process.* London: Taylor Graham.

Ding, H. (2007). Genre analysis of personal statements: Analysis of moves in application essays to medical and dental schools. *English for Specific Purposes, 26,* 368–392.

Feak, C. (2009). Negotiating publication: Author responses to peer review of medical research articles in thoracic surgery. *Revista Canaria de Estudios Ingleses, 59,* 17–34.

Gesuato, S. (2004). *Giving credit where credit is due: The case of acknowledgments in PhD dissertations.* PhD Dissertation, the University of California at Berkeley.

Giannoni, D. S. (2002). Worlds of gratitude: A contrastive study of acknowledgment texts in English and Italian research articles. *Applied Linguistics, 23,* 1–31.

Hyland, K. (2004). Graduates' gratitude: The generic structure of dissertation acknowledgments. *English for Specific Purposes 23,* 303–324.

Kirkpatrick, A. (1991). Information sequencing in Mandarin letters or requests. *Anthropological Linguistics, 33,* 183–203.

Meizlish, D., & Kaplan, M. (2008). Valuing and evaluating teaching in academic hiring: A multi-disciplinary, cross-institutional study. *Journal of Higher Education. 79,* 489–512.

Samraj, B., & Monk, L. (2008). The statement of purpose in graduate program applications: Genre structure and disciplinary variation. *English for Specific Purposes, 27,* 193–211.

Swales, J. M. (2004). *Research genres: Explorations and applications.* New York: Cambridge University Press.

Tardy, C. M., & Swales, J. M. (2011). "Genre Analysis" in *Pragmatics of Discourse.* London: Routledge.